Healthy
Smoothie
RECIPE BOOK

Healthy Smoothie

RECIPE BOOK

Easy

MIX-AND-MATCH

Smoothie Recipes For
A Healthier You

JENNIFER KOSLO, RD, CSSD

ROCKRIDGE
PRESS

This book is dedicated to my parents for their undying support of my endeavors and their never-ending enthusiasm to test my smoothies recipes.

For general information on our other products and services or to obtain technical support, please contact our Customer Care Department within the U.S. at (866) 744-2665, or outside the U.S. at (510) 253-0500.

Rockridge Press publishes its books in a variety of electronic and print formats. Some content that appears in print may not be available in electronic books, and vice versa.

TRADEMARKS: Rockridge Press and the Rockridge Press logo are trademarks or registered trademarks of Callisto Media Inc. and/or its affiliates, in the United States and other countries, and may not be used without written permission. All other trademarks are the property of their respective owners. Rockridge Press is not associated with any product or vendor mentioned in this book.

Front cover photo © Shannon Douglas. Back cover photo: Tanya Zouev/Stockfood.

Interior photos: Tatjana Ristanic/Stocksy, pg. 2; Laura Adani/Stocksy, pg. 6; Tanya Zouev/Stockfood, pg. 7; Ina Peters/Stocksy, pg. 9; Birgit Twellmann/Stockfood, pg. 24; Davide Illini/Stocksy, pg. 29; Ina Peters/Stocksy, pg. 43; Ina Peters/Stocksy, pg. 59; Valerie Janssen/Stockfood, pg. 75; Pavel Gramatikov/Stocksy, pg. 91; Ina Peters/Stocksy, pg. 107; Pavel Gramatikov/Stocksy, pg. 123; Pavel Gramatikov/Stocksy, pg. 137; Nataša Mandić/Stocksy, pg. 153; Nicole Young/Stocksy, pg. 167; Noemi Hauser/Stocksy, pg. 182.

ISBN: Print 978-1-62315-671-8 | eBook 978-1-62315-672-5

Contents

Introduction

Countless dietary trends boast miraculous claims that often don't hold up to scrutiny. But the ubiquitous smoothie? Sure they can be loaded with fiber, vitamins, minerals, and protein but can they really improve your health? Personally, including smoothies into my diet took my athletics and my health to the next level.

My love affair with smoothies started years ago in Fort Collins, Colorado, when I was in graduate school working towards my dual masters of nutrition and exercise science degrees and becoming a registered dietitian. I was also training hard with one of the best coaches in the country and competing in countless 10Ks, half marathons, marathons, and triathlons. I was a new vegetarian learning how to eat a nutritionally balanced diet. I must confess, a few areas needed improvement; my recovery from training was not optimal and my energy was low. During that time I was also working part-time at Alfalfa's Market and discovered their smoothie bar—something new at the time. Smoothies were foreign to me but at the coaxing of my co-workers I got adventurous. I tried out a few of their specialties with musical names like

Strawberry Fields, Blue Diva, and CaColorado. And guess what? They were phenomenal! Super thick, sweet, and loaded with nutrition. I was amazed by the difference they made in my energy level. I felt "supercharged." On the days I had smoothies I noticed a remarkable difference in my recovery from my long runs and speed work. I was instantly hooked on smoothie making and started experimenting at home with different fruits, liquids, bases, and add-ins.

What I like most about smoothie making is how they are the perfect venue for kicking your nutrition up a notch because they are highly customizable. Smoothies work well with the addition of a wide variety of supercharged add-ins like probiotics, omega-3 fats, grains, beans, nuts, and phytochemical-rich foods galore. They are also extremely versatile and can make a healthy breakfast, post-workout recovery drink, light lunch, and a hearty afternoon snack.

Lately, I've been experimenting with smoothie "bowls." They're a way to enjoy smoothies with a spoon instead of drinking them with a straw.

Smoothie bowls are thicker in consistency, and typically use toppings like granola, hemp seeds, or sliced nuts. You might find smoothie bowls to be a fun change from regular smoothies, especially if you are like me and enjoy eating things out of bowls.

I hope you enjoy the recipes in this book and make smoothies a regular part of your dietary routine.

Custom Smoothies for Vibrant Health

Finding the time and budget to eat healthy foods can be a challenge. More and more, Americans are consuming meals on the go, grabbing a quick bite between work, kids' activities, and other functions that keep them busy from dawn until dusk. • Commercially prepared foods geared towards eating on the go are often high in artificial ingredients, fat, sugar, and salt while containing insufficient nutrition. While these foods are convenient and cheap, they lack nutrient density. In other words, these foods may serve as a source of bulk and calories, without the vitamins and minerals necessary to sustain good health. • Enter the smoothie. The smoothies in this book are nutritionally dense; they're packed with the vitamins and minerals you need without blowing your caloric or financial budgets. They contain affordable ingredients, are easy to make, and are the perfect meal or snack when you're on the run.

10 Reasons Smoothies Support Good Health

If you want to be healthier, smoothies will definitely help. If you've never smoothied before, you're about to discover just how healthy these delicious foods can be.

1. **You increase your daily servings of fruits and vegetables.** According to the *Journal of the Academy of Nutrition and Dietetics,* most Americans don't consume the suggested daily intake for fruits and vegetables. Smoothies are a great way to add nutrient-dense fruits and veggies to your diet.

2. **You eat a wider variety of produce.** Smoothies are an especially good way to add healthy produce you don't enjoy to your diet. For example, if you can't stomach the flavor of superfood kale, but you really want the nutritional benefits that come with it, blending it with fruits in a smoothie can disguise the taste while allowing you the nutritional benefits of this dark, leafy green.

3. **You add fiber to your diet.** The Mayo Clinic notes that women need about 25 grams of fiber per day, while men need about 35 grams. Americans eat around 15 grams daily, well short of this goal. Fiber helps maintain the health of your bowels, fills you up, and has cardio-protective benefits, so it's important to well-being. Adding fibrous fruits, vegetables, and seeds (such as flax or chia) to smoothies can help bring you closer to the recommendations..

4. **You increase your antioxidant intake.** Antioxidants can help reduce cell damage that comes about from oxidative stress. Fruits and vegetables are antioxidant powerhouses, and consuming them may help reduce the risk of developing certain diseases.

5. **You increase your vitamin and mineral intake.** Even if you replace just one or two fast or processed food meals per week with smoothies, you'll be vastly improving your vitamin and mineral intake. That's because smoothies contain fruits and vegetables that are packed with nutrition, while processed and fast-food meals tend to be nutritionally bankrupt.

6. **You reduce your consumption of added sugars.** Americans eat a lot of added sugar, which adds calories without nutrients. Replacing sugary snacks with a healthy, sugar-free smoothie is a great way to reduce the amount of sugar you eat in your diet.

7. **You reduce your consumption of added salt.** According to the American Heart Association, about 75 percent of salt intake comes from processed and fast foods, so replacing them with more natural, salt-free foods such as smoothies may help reduce the risk of developing high blood pressure.

8. **You decrease your overall stress levels.** While drinking a smoothie won't help you feel less stressed, making smoothies a regular part of your diet can reduce your overall stress load. It's not the nutrients in smoothies that will do this, but rather the effect the smoothies will have on your lifestyle. You can save money with smoothies, and they are so quick and easy to prepare that they will save time in meal prep. You might even enjoy preparing and drinking smoothies as part of your daily ritual.

9. **You save calories.** Replacing fast- and processed-food meals with smoothies can help you save calories, depending on the smoothies you choose. Of course, smoothies can be high in calories as well, but by choosing low-fat, low-calorie ingredients along with healthful fruits and vegetables, you can replace a few high-calorie meals per week.

10. **You supplement your diet with a wider variety of nutrients.** While it's usually best to get your vitamins and minerals from the food you eat, it's not always feasible to cook perfect, nutrient-packed meals every day. This is where smoothies can help. In addition to "hiding" fruits and vegetables well, smoothies are also very easy to supplement with nutrition-boosting powders and liquids that add valuable nourishment when you're too busy to prepare more traditional meals.

While this book offers specific smoothie recipes, the great thing about it is just how easy it is to customize them. The recipes offer substitution suggestions, or you can venture out on your own. Using the charts and tables in this book, you can build your own smoothies, blending flavors like a pro and creating concoctions that meet your own unique nutritional needs.

For example, if you need a dairy-free smoothie, use a nondairy replacement for smoothies calling for milk. If you're concerned about calories, choose less caloric or lower-fat ingredients. If you want a spicier smoothie, add one of the spices suggested in the chart that follows. Whatever you choose, this book makes it super easy to tweak the flavor, texture, fiber content, caloric level, fat content, or makeup of any smoothie. Use the recipe as a jumping-off point to create your own versions that suit your needs.

Smoothie Basics

Making a smoothie sounds simple enough: just throw all of your ingredients in a blender and whiz it up until smooth. That technique may work some of the time, but if you want to make a healthy and tasty smoothie every time, use this go-to guide for making a smoothie in 7 easy steps.

Choose your recipe. It's always good to have a plan before you begin, so find a recipe you would like to make, base it on your health goals, and use the recipe labels (descriptions) in this book as guidance. Assemble your ingredients and prep them as needed ahead of time.

Add your liquid. Pour about one cup of liquid into the blender, or use the blades of the blender as a guide and add liquid until the tips are covered. Add more liquid for a thinner consistency and less if you like your smoothies to be thick.

Add your base. The base or "body" of your smoothie will add a creamy texture, bulk, and taste. Bases also make your smoothie more nutritious and can double as a source of protein. Creamy fruits like bananas, mangos, and peaches make great bases and add a sweet taste. Other good options are avocados, nut butters, tofu, yogurt, chia seed gel, cooked beans, and oats.

Add fruits and/or vegetables. Fruits add sweetness and texture along with fiber, vitamins, and minerals. Most fruit can be used fresh or frozen, so experiment and see what you prefer. If you are adding greens, start with neutral-tasting ones like spinach and kale and have fun exploring different fruit and vegetable combinations.

Optional add-ins. This is where your smoothie gets its character and where you can give it a nutrition and flavor boost. Add-ins include spices, protein powders, seeds, grains, and superfoods such as blueberries or spinach.

Blend until smooth. Start out on a low setting (if available) before turning up to top speed. Blend until the liquid is fully circulating for about 10 seconds. Depending on your ingredients and preference, total blend time is usually between 30 and 60 seconds.

Drink up! Lastly and most importantly, pour into a large container and enjoy!

Spicing Things Up

Do you want to spice up your smoothie? You're not alone. Spices are becoming increasingly popular in smoothies. Many people prize them for the pizazz they add to the smoothie, while others seek spices with specific potential health benefits to give their smoothie an extra health boost. Try the following.

ALLSPICE

FLAVOR: warm, slightly sweet, pungent, spicy

NUTRITIONAL VALUE: treats gas and indigestion

AMOUNT SUGGESTED: ⅛ teaspoon

PAIRINGS: fruit, squash, pumpkin

ANISE

FLAVOR: mild licorice

NUTRITIONAL VALUE: expectorant, diuretic, treats gas and indigestion

AMOUNT SUGGESTED: ⅛ teaspoon

PAIRINGS: fruit

CARDAMOM

FLAVOR: sweet, pungent, spicy

NUTRITIONAL VALUE: digestive aid, treats heartburn, treats gas

AMOUNT SUGGESTED: ⅛ teaspoon

PAIRINGS: bananas, apples, pears, pumpkin, squash, greens

CAYENNE

FLAVOR: hot, spicy

NUTRITIONAL VALUE: pain relief, thermogenic

AMOUNT SUGGESTED: a pinch or two

PAIRINGS: all fruits, all vegetables, all nuts and seeds

CEYLON CINNAMON
(not cassia cinnamon)

FLAVOR: warm, slightly sweet, spicy

NUTRITIONAL VALUE: antioxidants, anti-inflammatory, may improve blood lipid profiles, improves insulin sensitivity

AMOUNT SUGGESTED: ¼ teaspoon

PAIRINGS: most fruits, berries, nuts and seeds

CLOVES

FLAVOR: warm, bittersweet, pungent

NUTRITIONAL VALUE: expectorant, calms upset stomach, toothache

AMOUNT SUGGESTED: ⅛ teaspoon

PAIRINGS: apples, beets, pears, pumpkin, root vegetables, squash

CORIANDER

FLAVOR: lemony, slightly bitter

NUTRITIONAL VALUE: digestive tonic, gas, upset stomach

AMOUNT SUGGESTED: ¼ teaspoon

PAIRINGS: banana, apple, citrus

CUMIN

FLAVOR: warm, spicy, pungent, slightly bitter

NUTRITIONAL VALUE: digestive tonic, diarrhea, diuretic **AMOUNT SUGGESTED:** ¼ teaspoon

PAIRINGS: avocado, citrus, coconut, cucumber

FENNEL

FLAVOR: slightly sweet, licorice

NUTRITIONAL VALUE: treats heartburn and gas, treats cough

AMOUNT SUGGESTED: ⅛ to ¼ teaspoon

PAIRINGS: apple, celery, pear, banana, berries

FENUGREEK

FLAVOR: warm, slightly sweet, maple

NUTRITIONAL VALUE: anti-inflammatory, digestive aid, improves blood lipids

AMOUNT SUGGESTED: ⅛ teaspoon

PAIRINGS: apple, pear, banana, squash, pumpkin

GINGER

FLAVOR: hot, spicy, sweet, woody

NUTRITIONAL VALUE: treats nausea, digestive tonic, fights heartburn, expectorant

AMOUNT SUGGESTED: ¼ teaspoon

PAIRINGS: squash, root vegetables, apples, pears, citrus, banana, cucumber

MACE

FLAVOR: like nutmeg, only milder

NUTRITIONAL VALUE: antimicrobial, anti-inflammatory

AMOUNT SUGGESTED: ¼ teaspoon

PAIRINGS: fruits, squash, pumpkin, spinach

NUTMEG

FLAVOR: warm, sweet, spicy, intense

NUTRITIONAL VALUE: anti-inflammatory, antimicrobial

AMOUNT SUGGESTED: ¼ teaspoon

PAIRINGS: fruits, squash, pumpkin, spinach

PEPPERCORN
(black, white, pink, green)

FLAVOR: warm, spicy

NUTRITIONAL VALUE: expectorant, thermogenic, digestive aid

AMOUNT SUGGESTED: ⅛ to ¼ teaspoon

PAIRINGS: berries, cherries, vegetables

TURMERIC

FLAVOR: slightly bitter, pungent, similar to mild ginger but more pungent

NUTRITIONAL VALUE: anti-inflammatory, antioxidant

AMOUNT SUGGESTED: ⅛ teaspoon

PAIRINGS: citrus, root vegetables

VANILLA BEAN

FLAVOR: sweet, mild

NUTRITIONAL VALUE: treats gas

AMOUNT SUGGESTED: ¼ to ½ teaspoon

PAIRINGS: all fruits, nuts and seeds, coconut

The Mix-and-Match Charts

Use your imagination to create countless smoothie recipes with the help of the Mix-and-Match charts in this section. Experiment with various fruits and vegetables.

Ice is generally optional depending on your preferences and the proportions of frozen, fresh, and liquid ingredients you use. Start with 1 to 4 cubes for a thinner shake and 5 to 10 cubes for a thicker shake. Suggested amounts are a starting point for creating a 16-ounce smoothie and the measurements are not set in stone, so experiment to find exactly what you like.

Mix-and-Match Flavors & Textures

Do you like your smoothies sweet and smooth? Sweet and chunky? Perhaps you prefer less sugar and more spice. Use the chart in this section to address your tastes.

1	2	3	4
LIQUID	**TEXTURE**	**VEGETABLES & FRUITS**	**SUPPLEMENTS & ADD-INS**
Choose your liquid from this column. Start with 1 cup or fill your blender to the top of the blades.	*Add an ingredient from this column to enhance the texture of your smoothie. This is your base.*	*Pick one or more vegetables and fruits and add them to your blender.*	*Add one or more of these healthy add-ins to boost the flavor and nutrient profile.*

SWEET & SMOOTH

Vanilla almond milk	½ cup pureed pumpkin	½ cup dark leafy greens: spinach, kale, Swiss chard	1 to 2 tablespoons vanilla protein powder: whey, rice, pea, hemp, soy
Rice milk	½ cup cooked sweet potato	½ cup frozen peaches	1 teaspoon vanilla extract
Cashew milk	1 tablespoon nut butter	½ overripe banana	1 to 2 tablespoons cacao or cocoa
Soy milk	½ cup Greek yogurt	1 cored and peeled pear	
Hemp milk		½ cup frozen strawberries	
Kefir			
Coconut water			
Carrot juice			
100% fruit juice			

SWEET & CHUNKY

Coconut water	1 to 2 small cooked and peeled beets	½ cup dark leafy greens: spinach, kale, Swiss chard	1 to 2 tablespoons flavored protein powder: whey, rice, pea, hemp, soy
100% orange juice	½ cup frozen banana chunks	½ cup chopped celery or cucumber	1 to 2 tablespoons cacao or cocoa
Vanilla almond milk	1 to 2 tablespoons grated coconut	½ cup frozen blueberries	1 tablespoon pomegranate seeds
Rice milk	1 to 2 Medjool dates	½ cup frozen cherries	1 tablespoon raisins
Cashew milk		1 cored and chopped pear	
Soy milk		½ cup frozen mango	
Hemp milk			
Beet juice			
Cherry juice			

▶

► Mix-and-Match Flavors & Textures

1 LIQUID	**2** TEXTURE	**3** VEGETABLES & FRUITS	**4** SUPPLEMENTS & ADD-INS
Choose your liquid from this column. Start with 1 cup or fill your blender to the top of the blades.	*Add an ingredient from this column to enhance the texture of your smoothie. This is your base.*	*Pick one or more vegetables and fruits and add them to your blender.*	*Add one or more of these healthy add-ins to boost the flavor and nutrient profile.*

LOW-SUGAR & SMOOTH

Water	¼ avocado	½ cup dark leafy greens: spinach, kale, Swiss chard	1 to 2 tablespoons unsweetened protein powder: whey, rice, pea, hemp, soy
Unsweetened almond milk	1 tablespoon flax oil	½ cup pureed pumpkin	
Unsweetened rice milk	¼ cup cooked rice	2 chopped apricots	
Unsweetened cashew milk	½ cup unsweetened yogurt	½ cup frozen peaches	1 tablespoon chia seeds
Unsweetened soy milk	½ cup tofu	½ cup frozen strawberries	1 tablespoon hemp seeds
Unsweetened hemp milk			
Nonfat or low-fat milk			
Unsweetened herbal tea			

LOW-SUGAR & CHUNKY

Water	¼ cup rolled oats	½ cup chopped celery	1 to 2 tablespoons unsweetened protein powder: whey, rice, pea, hemp, soy
Unsweetened almond milk	¼ cup cooked beans	½ cup chopped cucumber	
Unsweetened rice milk	2 tablespoons sunflower seeds	½ cup dark leafy greens: spinach, kale, Swiss chard	
Unsweetened cashew milk	2 tablespoons almonds	½ cup frozen pomegranate seeds	1 teaspoon vanilla extract
Unsweetened soy milk		1 cored and chopped apple	
Unsweetened hemp milk			
Nonfat or low-fat milk			
Unsweetened herbal tea			

▶ Mix-and-Match Flavors & Textures

1
LIQUID

Choose your liquid from this column. Start with 1 cup or fill your blender to the top of the blades.

2
TEXTURE

Add an ingredient from this column to enhance the texture of your smoothie. This is your base.

3
VEGETABLES & FRUITS

Pick one or more vegetables and fruits and add them to your blender.

4
SUPPLEMENTS & ADD-INS

Add one or more of these healthy add-ins to boost the flavor and nutrient profile.

SPICY & SMOOTH

LIQUID	TEXTURE	VEGETABLES & FRUITS	SUPPLEMENTS & ADD-INS
Chai tea	1 to 2 tablespoons ground flaxseed	½ cup beet greens	1 to 2 tablespoons vanilla protein powder: whey, rice, pea, hemp, soy
Iced coffee	1 tablespoon nut butter	½ cup dandelion greens	¼ teaspoon ground nutmeg
Green tea	¼ avocado	½ cup dark leafy greens: spinach, kale, Swiss chard	¼ teaspoon ground cinnamon
Mint tea	½ cup tofu	½ cup frozen mango	1 teaspoon molasses
Yerba mate	½ cup yogurt	½ cup frozen banana	
Ginger tea			

SPICY & CHUNKY

LIQUID	TEXTURE	VEGETABLES & FRUITS	SUPPLEMENTS & ADD-INS
Chai tea	1 to 2 tablespoons toasted wheat germ	½ cup beet greens	1 to 2 tablespoons protein powder: whey, rice, pea, hemp, soy
Iced coffee	1 to 2 crushed ginger snaps	½ cup dandelion greens	1 teaspoon maca powder
Green tea	¼ cup granola	½ cup chopped cucumber	¼ teaspoon minced ginger
Mint tea	1 to 2 tablespoons cacao nibs	½ cup chopped celery	¼ teaspoon cloves
Yerba mate	2 tablespoons cashews	½ cup frozen banana	1 tablespoon fresh mint
Ginger tea		½ cup frozen strawberries	
		½ cup frozen cherries	

Mix-and-Match Nutrients

You may also want to customize your smoothie based on your nutrition and health goals, whether you want your smoothie to be a light snack, a workout recovery drink, a meal replacement, or a healthy treat. Use the Mix-and-Match chart in this section to customize your smoothie based on your unique nutritional needs.

1 LIQUID	2 VEGETABLES & FRUIT	3 PROTEIN	4 SUPPLEMENTS & ADD-INS
Choose your liquid from this column. Start with 1 cup or fill your blender to the top of the blades.	*Pick one or more vegetables and fruits and add them to your blender.*	*Pick one or more protein ingredients and add to your blender.*	*Provide an added nutritional boost by selecting one or more supplements and add-ins.*
LOW-FAT			
Water	½ cup dark leafy greens: spinach, kale, Swiss chard	½ cup nonfat Greek yogurt	1 to 2 tablespoons protein powder: whey, rice, pea, hemp, soy
Almond milk	½ cup chopped celery or cucumber	½ cup silken tofu	1 teaspoon vanilla extract
Rice milk	½ cup pureed pumpkin	½ cup beans	1 teaspoon maca
Cashew milk	½ cup frozen berries	2 tablespoons powdered peanut butter	1 teaspoon spirulina
Unsweetened teas	½ cup frozen banana		
Iced coffee	½ cup frozen mango		
Nonfat or low-fat milk			
Coconut water			
LOW-SUGAR			
Water	½ cup dark leafy greens: spinach, kale, Swiss chard	½ cup silken tofu	1 to 2 tablespoons unsweetened protein powder: whey, rice, pea, hemp, soy
Unsweetened almond milk	½ cup chopped celery or cucumber	1 to 2 tablespoons nut butter	½ teaspoon stevia
Unsweetened rice milk	½ cup pureed pumpkin	½ cup beans	1 teaspoon vanilla extract
Unsweetened soy milk	½ cup frozen berries	½ cup nonfat or low-fat cottage cheese	
Unsweetened cashew milk	¼ avocado		
Unsweetened teas	2 apricots		
Iced coffee	1 peeled and cored apple		
Nonfat or low-fat milk			

▶ Mix-and-Match Nutrients

1
LIQUID

Choose your liquid from this column. Start with 1 cup or fill your blender to the top of the blades.

2
VEGETABLES & FRUIT

Pick one or more vegetables and fruits and add them to your blender.

3
PROTEIN

Pick one or more protein ingredients and add to your blender.

4
SUPPLEMENTS & ADD-INS

Provide an added nutritional boost by selecting one or more supplements and add-ins.

LOW-CARB			
Water Unsweetened teas Iced coffee	½ cup dark leafy greens: spinach, kale, Swiss chard ½ cup chopped celery or cucumber ½ cup frozen berries 2 apricots ¼ avocado	½ cup nonfat Greek yogurt ½ cup silken tofu ½ cup nonfat or low-fat cottage cheese	1 to 2 tablespoons unsweetened protein powder: whey, rice, pea, hemp, soy ½ teaspoon stevia 1 teaspoon vanilla extract

HIGH-PROTEIN			
Nonfat or low-fat milk Soy milk Almond milk with added protein Nonfat or low-fat kefir	½ cup dark leafy greens: spinach, kale, Swiss chard ⅓ cup green peas ½ cup shelled edamame ½ cup frozen berries ½ cup frozen banana ½ cup frozen mango	½ cup silken tofu ½ cup Greek yogurt ½ cup beans 1 to 2 tablespoons nut butter ½ cup nonfat or low-fat cottage cheese	2 to 4 tablespoons protein powder: whey, rice, pea, hemp, soy 2 tablespoons wheat germ 2 tablespoons hemp seeds 2 tablespoons chia seeds 1 to 2 tablespoons cocoa

▶

▶ Mix-and-Match Nutrients

1
LIQUID

Choose your liquid from this column. Start with 1 cup or fill your blender to the top of the blades.

2
VEGETABLES & FRUIT

Pick one or more vegetables and fruits and add them to your blender.

3
PROTEIN

Pick one or more protein ingredients and add to your blender.

4
SUPPLEMENTS & ADD-INS

Provide an added nutritional boost by selecting one or more supplements and add-ins.

LOW-FAT & HIGH-PROTEIN

Nonfat or low-fat milk	½ cup dark leafy greens: spinach, kale, Swiss chard	½ cup silken tofu	2 to 4 tablespoons protein powder: whey, rice, pea, hemp, soy
Low-fat soy milk	⅓ cup green peas	½ cup cooked quinoa	2 tablespoons oats
Almond milk with added protein	½ cup shelled edamame	½ cup Greek yogurt	
Low-fat kefir	½ cup frozen berries	½ cup beans	
	½ cup frozen peaches	2 tablespoons powdered peanut butter	
	½ cup frozen cherries		

LOW-FAT & LOW-SUGAR

Water	½ cup dark leafy greens: spinach, kale, Swiss chard	½ cup silken tofu	1 to 2 tablespoons unsweetened protein powder: whey, rice, pea, hemp, soy
Unsweetened almond milk	½ cup chopped celery or cucumber	½ cup nonfat or low-fat Greek yogurt	½ teaspoon stevia
Unsweetened rice milk	½ cup frozen berries	½ cup beans	1 teaspoon vanilla extract
Unsweetened soy milk	½ cup frozen peaches	½ cup nonfat or low-fat cottage cheese	
Unsweetened cashew milk	2 apricots		
Unsweetened teas	1 peeled and cored apple		
Iced coffee			
Nonfat or low-fat milk			

▶ Mix-and-Match Nutrients

1
LIQUID

Choose your liquid from this column. Start with 1 cup or fill your blender to the top of the blades.

2
VEGETABLES & FRUIT

Pick one or more vegetables and fruits and add them to your blender.

3
PROTEIN

Pick one or more protein ingredients and add to your blender.

4
SUPPLEMENTS & ADD-INS

Provide an added nutritional boost by selecting one or more supplements and add-ins.

HIGH-PROTEIN & LOW-SUGAR

Nonfat or low-fat milk	½ cup dark leafy greens: spinach, kale, Swiss chard	½ cup silken tofu	2 to 4 tablespoons protein powder: whey, rice, pea, hemp, soy
Unsweetened soy milk	½ cup chopped celery or cucumber	½ cup plain Greek yogurt	2 tablespoons hemp seeds
Plain kefir	½ cup frozen berries	½ cup beans	2 tablespoons ground flaxseed
	½ cup frozen peaches	½ cup nonfat or low-fat cottage cheese	1 teaspoon vanilla extract
	2 apricots	½ cup cooked quinoa	1 teaspoon stevia
	1 peeled and cored apple		

HIGH-PROTEIN & LOW-CARB

Nonfat of low-fat milk	½ cup dark leafy greens: spinach, kale, Swiss chard	½ cup silken tofu	2 to 4 tablespoons protein powder: whey, rice, pea, hemp, soy
Unsweetened soymilk	⅓ cup green peas	½ cup plain Greek yogurt	2 tablespoons hemp seeds
Plain kefir	½ cup shelled edamame	2 tablespoons powdered peanut butter	2 tablespoons ground flaxseed
	½ cup frozen berries	½ cup nonfat or low-fat cottage cheese	1 teaspoon vanilla extract
	½ cup frozen peaches		1 teaspoon stevia
	2 apricots		
	1 peeled and cored apple		

Nourishing Ingredients & Convenient Substitutions

As you experiment with smoothie making you will learn the function of the various ingredients and be able to make substitutions on the fly. The following Mix-and-Match chart is meant to help you choose alternative ingredients when you may not have what a recipe calls for on hand. Most liquids work well in smoothies but avoid sugar-heavy fruit juices and pick 100% juice or juice your own. Using some type of milk adds creaminess, but filtered water is a great choice when you are watching calories and don't want the liquid to affect the flavor profile of your drink.

Try to include at least one "creamy" fruit such as banana, mango, peach, pear, apple, or papaya. Good combinations include banana and strawberry, apple and blueberry, and mango and pineapple. Greens like spinach add little to no taste and will give your smoothie a nutritional boost and add thickness. Try to add at least one protein and one healthy fat to avoid creating a "sugar bomb."

Have fun experimenting with different ingredients for added texture, flavor, and nutrition.

LIQUID

Ideal	More Convenient/ Cheaper Options
Nonfat or low-fat milk	Water
Kefir	Juice + water
Soy milk	Iced coffee
Almond milk	Herbal teas
Oat milk	Vinegar + water
Hemp milk	
Cashew milk	
Almond milk with added protein	
Rice milk	
Coconut milk	
Coconut water	
100% juice	

INGREDIENTS TO ADD TEXTURE

Ideal	More Convenient/ Cheaper Options
Avocado	Beans (cooked)
Chia seeds	Coconut (shredded)
Coconut flour	Cranberries (dried)
Rice (cooked)	Crushed ice
Flaxseed (ground)	Ginger snaps
Medjool dates	Graham crackers
Pomegranate seeds	Granola
Psyllium husk	Oat bran
Rice bran	Oat flour
	Rolled oats
	Wheat bran
	Wheat germ

FRUITS

Ideal	More Convenient/ Cheaper Options
Apples (peeled and cored)	Bananas (fresh; use less liquid and more ice)
Banana (frozen)	Citrus fruits
Berries: strawberries, cherries, blueberries, raspberries (frozen)	Fruits (canned; rinse in colander)
Mango (frozen)	Grapes
Pears (peeled and cored)	Kiwi
	Watermelon
	Substitute 2 veggies

VEGGIES

Ideal	More Convenient/ Cheaper Options
Baby beets (steamed)	Broccoli (frozen)
Beet greens	Cucumber (chopped)
Dark leafy greens (frozen): spinach, kale, chard	Celery (chopped)
Sweet potato (peeled, cubed, and steamed)	Greens (fresh; use less liquid and more ice)
	Substitute 2 fruits

HEALTHY FATS

Ideal	More Convenient/ Cheaper Options
Almond butter	Almonds
Avocados	Cashews
Chia seeds	Peanut butter
Flaxseed	Peanuts
Hemp seeds	Sunflower seeds
	Walnuts

SUPPLEMENTAL ADD-INS

Ideal	More Convenient/ Cheaper Options
Bee pollen	100% juice
Cacao nibs	Cranberries (dried)
Cacao powder	Extra dark leafy greens
Chia seeds	Herbs and spices (dried)
Chlorella	Vanilla (imitation)
Ginger (fresh, minced)	Wheat germ
Goji berries	
Herbs (fresh, chopped)	
Maca	
Salba seeds	
Spirulina	
Stevia	
Vanilla extract	
Wheatgrass	

PROTEINS

Ideal	More Convenient/ Cheaper Options
Greek yogurt	Beans (canned)
Shelled edamame	Cottage cheese
Silken tofu	Green peas (frozen)
Soy yogurt	Plain yogurt
Whey, rice, pea, soy, hemp protein powder	Ricotta cheese

Smoothie Troubleshooting

Whether you're making your first smoothie or are a seasoned pro, there are times when your drink just doesn't turn out the way you intended. This leaves you with a conundrum: do you pitch it down the drain, waste the ingredients, get aggravated, and write it off as a "live and learn" experience? Or, do you rise to the challenge and find a way to not only salvage it but turn it into the *best smoothie ever*? Personally I am not a fan of food waste so I prefer to rise to the challenge and hope you will too by trying the following tips and tricks.

OFF-PUTTING COLOR

Solution: While the color of a smoothie won't affect the vitamin and mineral content, we do eat with our eyes as well as our palate, so a brown smoothie may end up being used for compost. To keep your smoothie green, pair green vegetables and herbs like spinach, kale, broccoli, cucumber, and mint with green, yellow, or orange vegetables like kiwifruit, pears, green apples, pineapples, mangos, peaches, and apricots.

WATERY OR THIN CONSISTENCY

Solution: A couple of smoothie ingredients rank in the realm of magic. They will end all of your watery smoothie problems: xanthan gum and guar gum. Gums are a vegan and gluten-free way to thicken your smoothie without adding unnecessary calories, carbohydrates, and fats. Gums provide viscosity and volume, both have great thickening power, and a little goes a long way. You can use either xanthan or guar gum in smoothies, but together is even better as they seem to work together synergistically. There is a bit of trial and error involved, so start with ½ teaspoon of each or 1 teaspoon if just using one. Add gums right along with the rest of your smoothie ingredients. If you don't mind adding more calories to your drink, other great thickeners are frozen bananas, oats, nut butters, tofu, milk, and yogurt. Chia seeds are another great option as they form a gel when allowed to soak in liquid for a few minutes. Simply add them to your liquid and let them sit for about 15 minutes and then add your remaining ingredients.

GRAINY OR CHUNKY CONSISTENCY

Solution. If your smoothie is too chunky you might just need to blend it a bit longer. This can happen if your blender isn't high-powered, as it may not be able to handle whole ingredients like dates and large chunks of fruits and vegetables. The best solution in this case is to precut larger ingredients or grind them in a food processor before adding them to your smoothie. If your smoothie is grainy, this may be a result of using a protein powder in your shake. Protein powders vary widely in their ingredient quality, taste, and

texture so you may want to start with half the recommended serving until you find a consistency that you enjoy.

THICK CONSISTENCY

Solution. To make your smoothie less thick without watering down the taste, simply add more milk (cow, plant-, or nut-based). Start with ½ cup at a time until you get the desired consistency. Beware of using water to thin down a smoothie as it will water down the taste and then you will have two problems.

BITTERNESS

Solution. Certain ingredients like arugula and dandelion greens can overpower a smoothie with a distinctively bitter taste. The best solution is to use a mild-tasting fruit or vegetable to neutralize the bitterness followed by the addition of a strongly flavored fruit. Bananas and spinach tend to neutralize bad flavors and strawberries, pineapples, and mangoes add a nice sweet punch. Consider keeping a few of these ingredients on hand in your freezer for those times when you need to erase bad flavors.

SWEETNESS

Solution: If you find your smoothie is too sweet or too sugary, you might want to double-check your ingredients. Many plant- and nut-based milks and most yogurts and protein powders have sweeteners added and can turn your smoothie into a sugar bomb. To reduce the sweetness, add a flavor neutralizer like half a banana, some avocado, frozen spinach, a dash of lemon juice, or a few slices of pear. A dash of salt will also do the trick.

LACK OF FLAVOR OR SWEETNESS

Solution: Most smoothie recipes include enough fruit to sweeten them without having to add sugar. However, when that's not the case, many smoothie connoisseurs prefer Medjool dates as the best way to sweeten a smoothie naturally. This king of dates has a super-sweet caramel-like taste that works well with just about any smoothie ingredient. If you have a high-powered blender, remove the pit and toss the fruit in with the rest of the ingredients. Otherwise soak dates in a small amount of warm water and chop them finely before adding them to your liquid base. Other natural sweeteners are overripe bananas, and if all else fails, add a small amount of stevia, honey, or maple syrup.

SUBSTITUTING FRESH OR FROZEN PRODUCE

Solution: If a recipe calls for frozen fruits and frozen vegetables and all you have is fresh, the trick is to simply build the rest of your smoothie with ingredients that have a thicker consistency. For your liquid choose a type of milk (cow, plant-, or nut-based) over water; add yogurt, tofu, or cooked beans; use chia seeds or xanthan or guar gum; and toss in a few extra ice cubes. If you only have frozen fruits and vegetables on hand, simply replace ice with water and adjust the proportions of the bulkier ingredients you use.

Using the Recipes—Reading the Labels

The recipes in this book are organized into chapters based on their health properties. For example, you'll find chapters on weight-loss recipes, detoxification recipes, and anti-inflammatory smoothies. Likewise, the recipes all have labels that will help you determine how recipes will fit into various diets. You can refer to the recipe index at the back of the book to find recipes by label. The recipes may be labeled as explained as follows:

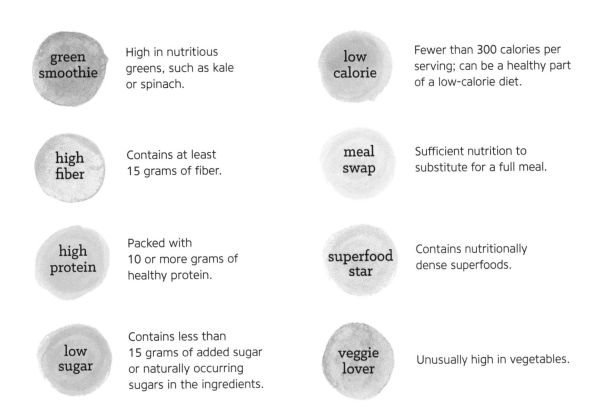

green smoothie — High in nutritious greens, such as kale or spinach.

low calorie — Fewer than 300 calories per serving; can be a healthy part of a low-calorie diet.

high fiber — Contains at least 15 grams of fiber.

meal swap — Sufficient nutrition to substitute for a full meal.

high protein — Packed with 10 or more grams of healthy protein.

superfood star — Contains nutritionally dense superfoods.

low sugar — Contains less than 15 grams of added sugar or naturally occurring sugars in the ingredients.

veggie lover — Unusually high in vegetables.

Detox and Cleanse

The term "detox" is a trendy word in health circles and is short for *detoxification*, which refers to removing and cleansing your body of toxins and environmental pollutants. Many detox diets are extremely low in calories, last for several days to a week, are hard to sustain, and leave you feeling fatigued and weak. They may even be dangerous. A better approach is get regular exercise, drink plenty of water, and detoxify your body a little bit every day by thoughtfully creating nutritious smoothies that include naturally purifying ingredients. The recipes in this chapter feature many of these ingredients, including lemons, cilantro, watermelon, ginger, dandelion greens, green tea, kale, avocado, apples, beets, yogurt, and more! You have lots of options when it comes to adding cleansing ingredients to your smoothies. Most add a nice flavor, while others can be hidden by more intensely flavored ingredients. Experiment with the following recipes and make them a part of your regular routine. That way, you can avoid drastic calorie-restricting detox diets.

Lemon-Lime Spinach Cleanser

Classic detox ingredients, lemon and lime combine in this refreshing and cleansing smoothie. The high vitamin C content of citrus fruits can aid digestion, stimulate the liver, and help aid in elimination. High in potassium, these alkalizing fruits get a fiber and chlorophyll boost with the addition of nutrient-rich spinach.

1 cup water
½ lemon, peeled and seeded
½ lime, peeled and seeded
1 medium frozen banana, sliced
2 cups baby spinach
1 pitted Medjool date
½ to 1 cup ice

Optional Add-Ins:

½ cup frozen blueberries
½ tablespoon fresh ginger, grated
2 tablespoons avocado

Combine all of the ingredients and blend until smooth. Serve right away.

Serves 1 | Per Serving: CALORIES: 177; TOTAL FAT: 1G; SUGAR: 24G; SODIUM: 50MG; CARBOHYDRATES: 46G; FIBER: 7G; PROTEIN: 4G

green smoothie

low calorie

If you like a thicker smoothie, choose frozen spinach instead of fresh. Frozen vegetables are processed when they are at peak nutrition and are a good option for reducing food waste.

For a thicker smoothie with more protein, use Greek yogurt in place of half of the coconut water. You could also include 2 tablespoons hemp seeds to add protein and keep this smoothie plant-based.

Peachy Endive

Tired of the same old spinach or kale smoothies? Then try endive instead! Endive is considered a natural diuretic that can promote intestinal regularity and balance your digestive system. Endive's naturally bitter taste blends well with the sweet peach and mango, offering a complex, earthy balance to this sweet and restorative smoothie.

1 cup coconut water
½ cup frozen mango
½ cup frozen peaches
2 cups endive
juice of ¼ lemon
1 tablespoon ground flaxseed
1 tablespoon chia seeds
½ to 1 cup ice

Optional Add-Ins:

½ frozen banana
1 apple, cored and sliced
¼ cup chopped avocado

Combine all of the ingredients and blend until smooth. Serve right away.

Serves 1 | Per Serving: CALORIES: 223; TOTAL FAT: 5G; SUGAR: 34G; SODIUM: 49MG; CARBOHYDRATES: 44G; FIBER: 10G; PROTEIN: 6G

Cilantro Mango Smoothie

From the same plant as coriander, cilantro is a good source of several minerals including potassium, calcium, magnesium, and iron. This antioxidant-rich herb has a fantastic flavor in addition to its antibacterial and antifungal actions. Add cilantro to any green smoothie that uses spinach or kale.

green smoothie

low calorie

1 cup coconut water
½ cup frozen mango
½ cup cilantro, stems removed
juice of ½ lime
1 teaspoon coconut oil
½ to 1 cup ice

Optional Add-Ins:

1 cup kale
½ frozen banana, sliced
1 teaspoon spirulina
2 tablespoons avocado

To make this smoothie a meal replacement, add a serving of Greek yogurt for protein, creaminess, and as a source of digestion-supporting probiotics.

Combine all of the ingredients and blend until smooth. Serve right away.

Serves 1 | Per Serving: CALORIES: 153; TOTAL FAT: 5G; SUGAR: 27G; SODIUM: 29MG; CARBOHYDRATES: 30G; FIBER: 2G; PROTEIN: 1G

green
smoothie

low
calorie

Ginger is among the healthiest (and most delicious) spices around. Fresh is best, but in a pinch, you can substitute with dried, ground ginger.

Ginger Watermelon Detox

Sweet and hydrating watermelon is a perfect ingredient for an invigorating and nourishing smoothie. Watermelon contains the amino acids citrulline and arginine, which can help increase blood flow, and is an excellent source of fiber for digestion, antioxidants, and vitamin C.

½ cup water
2 cups watermelon, chopped
½ cup frozen peaches
1 cup kale
juice of ½ lemon
1 teaspoon fresh ginger, grated
½ to 1 cup ice

Optional Add-Ins:

1 cup green grapes
pinch cayenne
½ cup Greek yogurt
2 tablespoons avocado

Combine all of the ingredients and blend until smooth. Serve right away.

Serves 1 | Per Serving: CALORIES: 169; TOTAL FAT: 1G; SUGAR: 26G; SODIUM: 38MG; CARBOHYDRATES: 40G; FIBER: 4G; PROTEIN: 5G

Minty Apple Fennel

If you are looking for variety in your green smoothies, give fennel a try! Fennel is a diuretic that is similar in flavor to licorice, and is an excellent source of fiber for heart and colon health. Rich in phytochemicals and vitamin C, the sweet taste of apple adds flavor and toxin-absorbing pectin.

1 cup water
1 cup kale
½ cup fresh mint, stems removed
1 cucumber, peeled and sliced
1 apple, cored and diced
1 cup fennel bulb, diced
¼ cup avocado, chopped
juice of ½ lemon
½ to 1 cup ice

Optional Add-Ins:

½ frozen banana
2 tablespoons ground flaxseed
1 teaspoon fresh ginger, minced
¼ cup fresh parsley, chopped

Combine all of the ingredients and blend until smooth. Serve right away.

Serves 1 | Per Serving: CALORIES: 300; TOTAL FAT: 9G; SUGAR: 25G; SODIUM: 102MG; CARBOHYDRATES: 57G; FIBER: 15G; PROTEIN: 8G

green smoothie

low calorie

veggie lover

high fiber

Cranberries are known to offer protection against urinary infections. Consider adding a ½ cup to boost the detox power of this smoothie.

Replace the pomegranate juice with water to decrease the sugar content and sweeten with a fiber-rich Medjool date, or try using no-calorie sweetener made from the stevia plant.

Very Berry Detox

Cherries, blueberries, raspberries, strawberries, cranberries, blackberries—take your pick as each type offers a unique array of powerful antioxidants and phytochemicals to support health. Simple and nutritious, this detoxifier has protein, fiber, ample vitamins and minerals, as well as omega-3 fats.

½ cup pomegranate juice
½ cup silken tofu
1 cup baby spinach
1 cup frozen berries
½ frozen banana, sliced
2 tablespoons ground flaxseed
½ to 1 cup ice

Optional Add-Ins:

1 orange, peeled and diced
1 teaspoon spirulina
juice of ½ lime

Combine all of the ingredients and blend until smooth. Serve right away.

Serves 1 | Per Serving: CALORIES: 341; TOTAL FAT: 8G; SUGAR: 35G; SODIUM: 64MG; CARBOHYDRATES: 56G; FIBER: 11G; PROTEIN: 11G

Pineapple Watercress Green Tea

This smoothie uses an all-star line-up of cleansing and detoxifying ingredients. Green tea is rich in the antioxidant EGCG, which protects your cells from damage, and pineapple contains the natural digestive enzyme bromelain, adding a wonderful sweet flavor. Neutral-tasting watercress is added to boost circulation and oxygenate tissues.

1 cup brewed and chilled green tea
1 cup loosely packed watercress
1 cup baby kale
½ cup frozen pineapple
½ frozen banana, sliced
¼ cup avocado, chopped
juice of 1 lemon
1 tablespoon fresh ginger, minced
½ to 1 cup ice

Optional Add-Ins:

½ cup silken tofu
2 tablespoons hemp seeds
stevia (optional)

Combine all of the ingredients and blend until smooth. Serve right away.

Serves 1 | Per Serving: CALORIES: 245; TOTAL FAT: 8G; SUGAR: 20G; SODIUM: 60MG; CARBOHYDRATES: 41G; FIBER: 8G; PROTEIN: 5G

veggie lover

green smoothie

low calorie

superfood star

Beware of adding pineapple to smoothies containing dairy products. The high acid content of the fruit can curdle the milk. Instead, choose soy yogurt or silken tofu for added protein.

green smoothie

veggie lover

For a red velvety–tasting smoothie, replace the coconut water with almond milk and add a pitted Medjool date and 1 tablespoon cocoa. These are perfect accompaniments to beets and cherries.

Beet Cherry Detox

When you think of green smoothies you may not think red beets, however beets are a great source of antioxidants, fiber, and iron. Avocado gives the smoothie a creamy texture and adds healthy fats, while sweet cherries and coconut water turn this into a delicious nutrient-rich treat.

1 cup coconut water
1 cup beet greens
½ cup cooked beets, chopped
½ cup frozen cherries
¼ cup avocado, chopped
1 stalk celery
2 tablespoons hemp seeds
½ to 1 cup ice

Optional Add-Ins:

1 tablespoon unsweetened cacao or cocoa
¼ cup rolled oats
1 cup kale, fresh or frozen

Combine all of the ingredients and blend until smooth. Serve right away.

Serves 1 | Per Serving: CALORIES: 303; TOTAL FAT: 15G; SUGAR: 29G; SODIUM: 193MG; CARBOHYDRATES: 38G; FIBER: 8G; PROTEIN: 9G

Kiwi Cleanser

Packed with more vitamin C than an orange, the creamy flesh of the kiwifruit is rich in cleansing dietary fiber. Kiwi is bursting with antioxidants and phytochemicals for optimal health. With its mild taste, kiwifruit makes a great addition to any green smoothie.

¾ cup water
2 kiwifruit, peeled and halved
½ apple, cored and chopped
½ frozen banana, sliced
2 cups baby kale
2 tablespoons chia seeds
½ to 1 cup ice

Optional Add-Ins:

½ tablespoon coconut oil
1 tablespoon coconut flakes
dash of salt
stevia or honey (optional)

If you don't have chia seeds on hand, replace with an equal amount of ground flaxseed, hemp seeds, avocado, coconut flour, or shelled edamame.

Combine all of the ingredients and blend until smooth. Serve right away.

Serves 1 | Per Serving: CALORIES: 308; TOTAL FAT: 6G; SUGAR: 29G; SODIUM: 63MG; CARBOHYDRATES: 66G; FIBER: 15G; PROTEIN: 10G

fiber

If apple cider vinegar
has too strong a flavor for
you, simply omit it and
replace it with the juice of
half a lemon.

Rejuvenating
Orange Strawberry

This smoothie has everything you need to receive extra energy
when you are feeling drained or need help getting through
a long winter day. Apple cider vinegar benefits the skin and
digestion, oranges and coconut water add a boost of cleansing
hydration and antioxidants, and turmeric adds a bit of
earthiness and an anti-inflammatory kick.

1 cup coconut water
2 tablespoons apple cider vinegar
2 navel oranges, peeled
½ cup frozen strawberries
½ frozen banana
1 tablespoon chia seeds
¼ teaspoon turmeric
1 teaspoon honey
½ to 1 cup ice

Optional Add-Ins:
1 tablespoon hemp seeds
½ cup silken tofu
1 to 2 cups dark leafy greens

Combine all of the ingredients and blend until smooth.
Serve right away.

Serves 1 | Per Serving: CALORIES: 369; TOTAL FAT: 3G; SUGAR: 67G;
SODIUM: 28MG; CARBOHYDRATES: 88G; FIBER: 15G; PROTEIN: 6G

Carrot Kale Detox

This veggie-rich smoothie contains ample phytonutrients and antioxidants to counteract the effects of overdoing it on less-than-healthy foods and drinks. High in potassium and fiber, this combination will help flush out sodium and restore normal hydration status. High in vitamin C, this light and refreshing smoothie will recharge your body.

1 cup water
½ frozen banana, sliced
¼ cup chopped avocado
2 cups kale
½ cup carrots, chopped
1 teaspoon grated fresh ginger
1 tablespoon chopped fresh parsley
1 teaspoon lime juice
1 tablespoon ground flaxseed
½ to 1 cup ice

Optional Add-Ins:
2 tablespoons hemp seeds
½ cup silken tofu
½ cup white beans

Combine all of the ingredients and blend until smooth. Serve right away.

Serves 1 | Per Serving: CALORIES: 260; TOTAL FAT: 10G; SUGAR: 10G; SODIUM: 103MG; CARBOHYDRATES: 40G; FIBER: 10G; PROTEIN: 7G

veggie lover

green smoothie

low sugar

low calorie

For an extra boost of potassium and electrolytes, use coconut water in place of half or all of the water. Or for added protein, try soy milk or protein-fortified almond milk.

Inflammation Fighters

Inflammation is part of the body's natural immune response, providing protection from foreign invaders such as microbes, plant pollen, and chemicals. But when it's out of control and persists on a day-to-day basis, it can damage the body and play a part in the development of rheumatoid arthritis, obesity, heart disease, and cancer. The good news is that the most powerful tools to fight inflammation don't come from the pharmacy, but from the grocery store. Consistently choosing foods known to reduce inflammation is the best way to reduce your risk, and making a smoothie chock-full of anti-inflammatory foods is a delicious and convenient way to incorporate these items. Some standout foods that combat inflammation are dark leafy greens, omega-3 fats, nuts and seeds, whole grains, all types of berries, pineapple, teas, and herbs such as ginger and turmeric. Never had a smoothie with turmeric before? You might be surprised at how good it tastes. Challenge yourself to try the recipes in this chapter. Use the Mix-and-Match charts in chapter 1. Experiment with the optional add-ins and substitution tips in order to customize the recipes for your health and nutrition goals.

Peachy Inflammation Fighter

The vibrant yellow color of this smoothie comes from the pigment curcumin, found in the spice turmeric. Curcumin has been shown in research to block chemicals in your body that produce inflammation and can be especially helpful for people with rheumatoid arthritis.

1 cup unsweetened almond milk
¼ cup avocado
1 cup frozen peaches
1 teaspoon turmeric
½ teaspoon ground ginger
1 teaspoon cinnamon
⅛ teaspoon black pepper
1 tablespoon chia seeds
1 to 2 pitted Medjool dates
½ to 1 cup ice

Optional Add-Ins:

½ frozen banana
1 to 2 cups dark leafy greens
¼ teaspoon garlic

Combine all of the ingredients and blend until smooth.
Serve right away.

To make this a meal replacement and up the inflammation-fighting power of the ingredients, add a serving of phytoestrogen-rich shelled edamame or soy yogurt.

Serves 1 | Per Serving: CALORIES: 346; TOTAL FAT: 14G; SUGAR: 44G; SODIUM: 184MG; CARBOHYDRATES: 69G; FIBER: 13G; PROTEIN: 6G

high protein

superfood star

When left unpeeled, fresh ginger can be stored in your refrigerator for at least three weeks or in your freezer for six months. Out of fresh? Substitute 1 teaspoon ground ginger.

Ginger Cranberry Anti-Inflammatory

This smoothie gets its kick from fresh ginger, a spice with anti-inflammatory powers that rival those of NSAIDs. A spice I recommend keeping on hand at all times, ginger teams up with inflammation-reducing cranberries, leafy greens, and omega-3 fats to address inflammation head-on.

1 cup water
½ frozen banana, sliced
1 cup frozen cranberries
1 tablespoon fresh ginger, peeled and chopped
2 cups fresh kale (or ½ cup frozen)
1 cup chopped celery
2 tablespoons hemp seeds
1 teaspoon honey
½ to 1 cup ice

Optional Add-Ins:

½ apple, cored and chopped
1 tablespoon ground flaxseed
½ cup Greek yogurt

Combine all of the ingredients and blend until smooth. Serve right away.

Serves 1 | Per Serving: CALORIES: 309; TOTAL FAT: 8G; SUGAR: 19G; SODIUM: 141MG; CARBOHYDRATES: 53G; FIBER: 10G; PROTEIN: 11G

Restorative Raspberry

Berries and nuts are an integral part of an inflammation-reducing diet, and new research shows that if you want a little sweetness in your life, molasses is a good choice. Rich in the mineral magnesium, antioxidants, and compounds that block inflammation, molasses adds extra sweetness to this very "berry-licious" smoothie.

high fiber

1 cup almond milk
1 cup frozen raspberries
¼ cup canned pumpkin
2 tablespoons walnuts
1 tablespoon ground flaxseed
1 teaspoon cinnamon
1 teaspoon molasses
½ to 1 cup ice

Optional Add-Ins:
½ teaspoon ground nutmeg
½ teaspoon ground ginger
1 cup leafy greens

Combine all of the ingredients and blend until smooth.
Serve right away.

Other nuts that are excellent for reducing inflammation include almonds and cashews. You can also substitute whole nuts with 2 tablespoons of nut butter.

Serves 1 | Per Serving: CALORIES: 497; TOTAL FAT: 15G; SUGAR: 67G; SODIUM: 171MG; CARBOHYDRATES: 89G; FIBER: 18G; PROTEIN: 9G

Balancing Blueberry

Boosting your fiber intake from whole grains like rolled oats can also reduce inflammation in the body. And while many people steer clear of soy, anti-inflammatory diets should emphasize plant proteins over animal. Soy contains complete high-quality protein in addition to a number of phytonutrients.

This smoothie is highly customizable. Have fun using your favorite berry, quinoa instead of oats, kale in place of spinach, and walnuts in place of sesame seeds.

1 cup soy milk
1 cup frozen blueberries
¼ cup rolled oats
2 tablespoons sesame seeds
2 cups fresh baby spinach (or ½ cup frozen)
1 teaspoon cinnamon
½ to 1 cup ice

Optional Add-Ins:

¼ cup avocado
1 serving hemp protein
½ teaspoon ground ginger

Combine all of the ingredients and blend until smooth. Serve right away.

Serves 1 | Per Serving: CALORIES: 415; TOTAL FAT: 15G; SUGAR: 25G; SODIUM: 177MG; CARBOHYDRATES: 59G; FIBER: 12G; PROTEIN: 17G

Strawberry Beet Strengthener

This earthy smoothie has a zesty flavor and creamy consistency. It's full of ingredients that will kick inflammation to the curb. Root vegetables like beets have high concentrations of antioxidants and anti-inflammatory properties, plus a number of vitamins and minerals for immune function. Enjoy this smoothie with a dollop of Greek yogurt on top and a sprinkle of goji berries.

½ cup almond milk
½ cup 100% orange juice
½ cup beets, cooked and sliced
1 cup beet greens
1 cup frozen strawberries
½ teaspoon turmeric
½ teaspoon ground ginger
¼ cup cashews
½ to 1 cup ice

Optional Add-Ins:

1 tablespoon goji berries
1 tablespoon chia seeds
½ frozen banana

Combine all of the ingredients and blend until smooth.
Serve right away.

Serves 1 | Per Serving: CALORIES: 385; TOTAL FAT: 18G; SUGAR: 32G; SODIUM: 239MG; CARBOHYDRATES: 53G; FIBER: 8G; PROTEIN: 9G

superfood
star

If you aren't familiar with turmeric, don't go overboard as it has a bitter taste. Adding frozen mango or banana can lessen the bite.

superfood
star

low
calorie

Fresh, canned, and frozen pineapple all provide the great anti-inflammatory and pain reduction benefits. However, if buying canned, be wary of added sugars in the liquid and remember to rinse before using.

Pain-Reducing Pineapple Ginger

Aside from tasting delicious, pineapple is an excellent source of free radical–fighting vitamin C and the protein-digesting enzyme bromelain, a natural anti-inflammatory agent especially beneficial for reducing pain and swelling in the joints. Enjoy this spicy, colorful smoothie as a nutritious way to start your day.

1 cup brewed and chilled green tea
1 cup pineapple, cut into chunks
½ frozen banana, sliced
2 tablespoons raw walnuts
½ teaspoon ground turmeric
½ teaspoon ground ginger
1 tablespoon ground flaxseed
½ to 1 cup ice

Optional Add-Ins:

1 teaspoon bee pollen
1 teaspoon rosehip powder
1 serving hemp protein
pinch cinnamon

Combine all of the ingredients and blend until smooth. Serve right away.

Serves 1 | Per Serving: CALORIES: 275; TOTAL FAT: 12G; SUGAR: 24G; SODIUM: 6MG; CARBOHYDRATES: 40G; FIBER: 7G; PROTEIN: 7G

Blueberry Basil Anti-Inflammatory

If you are feeling adventurous, skip the pesto and try this smoothie made with antioxidant-rich basil. The highly fragrant leaves of basil contain both powerful volatile oils that reduce inflammation and free radical–fighting flavonoids. Mix things up and enjoy the sweet and savory flavors of this smoothie.

1 cup almond milk
1 cup frozen blueberries
½ frozen banana, sliced
5 to 7 large basil leaves
1 tablespoon tahini
2 tablespoons hemp seeds
2 cups dark leafy greens (or ½ cup frozen)
½ to 1 cup ice

Optional Add-Ins:

½ cup soy yogurt
1 serving protein powder of your choice
¼ cup rolled oats

Combine all of the ingredients and blend until smooth. Serve right away.

Serves 1 | Per Serving: CALORIES: 384; TOTAL FAT: 18G; SUGAR: 29G; SODIUM: 226MG; CARBOHYDRATES: 49G; FIBER: 9G; PROTEIN: 12G

Oats are a surprisingly good source of protein, with about 6 grams per ½ cup. If you like your smoothies thick, soak your oats overnight in the almond milk for a creamy textured delight.

↘ Coconut water is
different from coconut
milk. Coconut milk,
especially the low-fat
variety, can be used in
moderation, but beware
that regular coconut milk
contains a significant
amount of saturated fat.

Papaya Coconut Inflammation Fighter

Papaya is rich in many vitamins and minerals, but its main pain-reducing component is an enzyme called papain. Paired with the enzyme power of pineapple and the omega-3 punch of chia seeds, this refreshing, tropical tasting drink is as nutritious as it is delicious.

½ cup coconut water
½ cup silken tofu
1 cup ripe papaya
½ cup chopped pineapple
2 tablespoons chia seeds
1 pitted Medjool date
½ to 1 cup ice

Optional Add-Ins:

¼ cup rolled oats
1 teaspoon coconut oil
2 tablespoons grated coconut
1 to 2 cups dark leafy greens

Combine all of the ingredients and blend until smooth. Serve right away.

Serves 1 | Per Serving: CALORIES: 271; TOTAL FAT: 7G; SUGAR: 40G; SODIUM: 108MG; CARBOHYDRATES: 52G; FIBER: 10G; PROTEIN: 8G

Cherry Rooibos

The inflammation-fighting force of this smoothie is off the charts! In a liquid base of antioxidant-rich rooibos tea, cherries contribute the potent pain-reducing and recovery-boosting phytochemicals quercitin and anthocyanin. With an added kick from spices, this creamy smoothie makes a great post-workout drink.

1 cup brewed and chilled rooibos tea
½ cup frozen cherries
½ cup frozen papaya
¼ cup avocado
2 tablespoons hemp seeds
½ teaspoon turmeric
½ teaspoon ground ginger
½ teaspoon cinnamon
¼ teaspoon cayenne
1 pitted Medjool date
½ to 1 cup ice

Optional Add-Ins:

1 to 2 cups dark leafy greens (or ½ cup frozen)
½ frozen banana
½ cup frozen blueberries
1 teaspoon coconut oil

Combine all of the ingredients and blend until smooth. Serve right away.

Serves 1 | Per Serving: CALORIES: 302; TOTAL FAT: 15G; SUGAR: 29G; SODIUM: 10MG; CARBOHYDRATES: 41G; FIBER: 8G; PROTEIN: 8G

superfood star

Teas are an outstanding source of phytochemicals and antioxidants; each type has a unique array of nutrients. Use your favorite flavor in place of the rooibos.

superfood
star

low
calorie

↘ You will need to freeze your orange ahead of time. Peel a bunch of very ripe and juicy oranges, quarter into large segments, freeze, and add to citrus smoothies for a sweet frosty flavor.

Coconut Carrot

When it comes to fighting inflammation, "green" isn't the only star. Golden fruits, veggies, and spices bring golden wellness to this smoothie. Carrots are full of vitamin A; oranges contain vitamin C, potassium, folate, and fiber; and turmeric tops the charts in healing and anti-inflammatory properties. Just be certain to freeze your orange first for best results.

1 cup unsweetened vanilla almond milk
1 large frozen orange, peeled and sliced
½ frozen banana
½ cup carrots, chopped
1 teaspoon coconut oil
1 tablespoon chia seeds
1 teaspoon turmeric powder
pinch ground cinnamon
pinch cayenne
½ teaspoon maple syrup
½ to 1 cup ice

Optional Add-Ins:

1 tablespoon shredded coconut
½ cup Greek yogurt
¼ cup chopped avocado

Combine all of the ingredients and blend until smooth. Serve right away.

Serves 1 | Per Serving: CALORIES: 288; TOTAL FAT: 11G; SUGAR: 30G; SODIUM: 220MG; CARBOHYDRATES: 49G; FIBER: 12G; PROTEIN: 6G

Pineapple Cherry Pain Fighter

Whole foods offer significant health benefits and can be an effective way to support your body's own natural healing abilities. Whether you have exercised strenuously or injured yourself, this smoothie combines some of the most powerful inflammation-fighting foods, including cherries, pineapple, hemp, and ginger, into one yummy drink.

½ cup water
½ cup 100% tart cherry juice
1 cup frozen pineapple
⅓ cup chopped avocado
1 serving hemp protein powder
2 cups baby spinach
1 teaspoon grated fresh ginger
½ teaspoon turmeric
⅛ teaspoon ground black pepper
stevia (optional)
½ to 1 cup ice

Optional Add-Ins:

½ frozen banana
1 tablespoon chia seeds
½ cup frozen cherries

Combine all of the ingredients and blend until smooth. Serve right away.

Serves 1 | Per Serving: CALORIES: 437; TOTAL FAT: 13G; SUGAR: 50G; SODIUM: 89MG; CARBOHYDRATES: 71G; FIBER: 11G; PROTEIN: 11G

high protein

superfood star

Using hemp protein provides a more concentrated source of inflammation-fighting omega-3 fats with the bonus of protein and fiber. Replace hemp protein powder with 2 tablespoons of hemp seeds for similar benefits.

veggie
lover

high
protein

superfood
star

↘ Oats are included for their anti-inflammatory properties and to add texture. You can substitute any leftover grains you have, such as quinoa, brown rice, millet, or amaranth.

Cucumber Arugula Inflammation Reducer

Arugula is a nutritious green that adds a peppery flavor and wonderful dimension to smoothies. High in B vitamins and vitamin K, arugula contains several powerful phytochemicals that have been shown to suppress inflammation in the body.

1 cup water
½ cup Greek yogurt
1 cup arugula
1 cup spinach
¼ cup chopped cucumber
⅓ cup pineapple
½ cup frozen mango
2 tablespoons almonds
¼ cup rolled oats
½ teaspoon ground cinnamon
½ teaspoon ground turmeric
½ teaspoon ground ginger
½ to 1 cup ice

Optional Add-Ins:
¼ cup chopped avocado
2 tablespoons chia seeds
½ cup berries
½ frozen banana

Combine all of the ingredients and blend until smooth. Serve right away.

Serves 1 | Per Serving: CALORIES: 306; TOTAL FAT: 8G; SUGAR: 23G; SODIUM: 72MG; CARBOHYDRATES: 46G; FIBER: 8G; PROTEIN: 19G

Kiwi Spinach Chia

A vitamin C star, sweet kiwifruit offers premier antioxidant protection due to its ability to neutralize free radicals, and as part of a healthy diet may offer protection against macular degeneration. With the added benefit of vitamin K–rich spinach and omega-3 fats, this delicious smoothie is one health-promoting mix.

1 cup unsweetened almond milk
½ frozen banana, sliced
2 cups baby spinach
2 ripe kiwis, peeled, cut into chunks
2 tablespoons chia seeds
1 tablespoon walnuts
1 pitted Medjool date
½ to 1 cup ice

Optional Add-Ins:

1 tablespoon wheatgrass powder
1 teaspoon flax oil
1 teaspoon maca powder
½ cup Greek yogurt

Combine all of the ingredients and blend until smooth. Serve right away.

When selecting kiwifruits, hold them between your thumb and forefinger and gently apply pressure; those that have the sweetest taste will yield gently.

Serves 1 | Per Serving: CALORIES: 371; TOTAL FAT: 14G; SUGAR: 37G; SODIUM: 233MG; CARBOHYDRATES: 65G; FIBER: 16G; PROTEIN: 10G

Weight Loss and Diabetes

It's easy to get carried away with adding ingredients to your smoothies because they are so adaptable, delicious, and healthy, and portion sizes don't really matter, right? Not exactly. Healthy foods have calories too and they count just as much as any other calorie. The good news is that you're in control of the type and amount of ingredients you use, and by keeping a few key tips in mind, you can make a diabetic-friendly smoothie that can help you reach your weight-loss goals. Some tips to keep in mind: Make your smoothie thick so that it fills you up while you are cutting calories; use low-fat or nonfat milks, water, or coconut water for the liquid and skip the juices; add protein to make it filling; add fiber and healthy carbs from fruits and veggies; add one tablespoon of healthy fats; go easy on sweeteners; and add natural blood sugar balancing and weight-loss aids such as cinnamon and green tea.

Sweet Strawberry Spinach

Low-calorie strawberries and slow-digesting protein give your weight loss efforts a boost in this tasty smoothie. Thickened by high-fiber avocados and protein-rich chia seeds, this smoothie provides ample healthy fats to keep you feeling full and satisfied for hours.

½ cup water
6 ounces plain nonfat Greek yogurt
½ cup frozen strawberries
½ cup frozen spinach (or 2 cups fresh)
1 tablespoon chia seeds
2 tablespoons chopped avocado
½ teaspoon vanilla extract
stevia (optional)
½ to 1 cup ice

Optional Add-Ins:

1 tablespoon psyllium husk
1 serving protein powder of your choice
¼ tablespoon ground cinnamon
2 tablespoons almonds

Combine all of the ingredients and blend until smooth. Serve right away.

Serves 1 | Per Serving: CALORIES: 191; TOTAL FAT: 6G; SUGAR: 12G; SODIUM: 74MG; CARBOHYDRATES: 19G; FIBER: 6G; PROTEIN: 19G

low sugar

low calorie

high protein

For a creamier smoothie, make chia gel. Combine one part chia seeds to one part water in a small container and let sit for 15 to 20 minutes. Refrigerate afterwards for use in smoothies for the next several weeks.

calorie

high
protein

A key ingredient for providing satiety and stabilizing blood sugar is a source of protein. If you aren't a fan of tofu, simply substitute Greek yogurt, cottage cheese, or a serving of your favorite protein powder.

Spiced Pear and Green Tea

Cayenne pepper and green tea are two of the best natural herbs for weight loss. Capsaicin and EGCG, the main active ingredients, are natural thermogenic chemicals that help speed up your metabolism and decrease your appetite. Paired with creamy pear and banana, this sweet and spicy mix is sure to satisfy.

1 cup brewed and chilled green tea
½ cup silken tofu
1 small pear, skin on, cut into small pieces
½ frozen banana, sliced into rounds
2 tablespoons ground flaxseed
⅛ teaspoon cayenne
2 tablespoons lemon juice
½ to 1 cup ice

Optional Add-Ins:

1 tablespoon honey
½ cup frozen kale
pinch cinnamon
½ cup strawberries

Combine all of the ingredients and blend until smooth. Serve right away.

Serves 1 | Per Serving: CALORIES: 266; TOTAL FAT: 7G; SUGAR: 23G; SODIUM: 43MG; CARBOHYDRATES: 41G; FIBER: 10G; PROTEIN: 10G

Apple Cashew

Apples and nuts make a perfect pairing in smoothies, providing fiber, protein, and slow-digesting carbs. Apples are rich in a type of fiber called pectin that forms a gel in your stomach, slowing down digestion and keeping your blood sugar steady. Creamy cashews add heart-healthy monounsaturated fats resulting in a sinfully delicious, filling shake.

¾ cup plain soymilk
1 serving protein powder (whey, hemp, pea, rice, soy)
½ cup frozen peaches
1 medium apple, peeled and chopped
1 tablespoon cashew butter
1 teaspoon apple pie spice
½ to 1 cup ice

Optional Add-Ins:

½ cup frozen spinach
1 tablespoon ground flaxseed
1 teaspoon vanilla extract
1 teaspoon cinnamon

Combine all of the ingredients and blend until smooth. Serve right away.

Serves 1 | Per Serving: CALORIES: 438; TOTAL FAT: 15G; SUGAR: 33G; SODIUM: 210MG; CARBOHYDRATES: 50G; FIBER: 7G; PROTEIN: 33G

high protein

Substitution Tip: You can substitute any nut or nut butter for the cashews. Some of the best picks for optimal nutrition are walnuts, almonds, and pistachios. Substitute 2 tablespoons whole nuts for 1 tablespoon nut butter.

protein

high
fiber

If you don't have flax oil on hand, substitute 2 tablespoons ground flaxseed. Not ready to commit to a full package? Check the bulk section of your local grocer.

Berry Metabolism Booster

This smoothie provides a hefty dose of vitamins, minerals, fiber, protein, and healthy fats to create a nutrient-rich filling meal. Cinnamon is a spice that has been shown to help stabilize blood sugar levels, and its rich taste compliments the sweetness of the blueberries and the tang of Greek yogurt.

¾ cup brewed and chilled green tea
6 ounces nonfat plain Greek yogurt
½ cup frozen broccoli florets
½ cup frozen blueberries
1 teaspoon flax oil
¼ cup garbanzo beans
¼ cup shelled pistachios
¼ teaspoon cinnamon
½ to 1 cup ice

Optional Add-Ins:

½ frozen banana
1 tablespoon psyllium husk
1 teaspoon nutmeg

Combine all of the ingredients and blend until smooth. Serve right away.

Serves 1 | Per Serving: CALORIES: 520; TOTAL FAT: 18G; SUGAR: 29G; SODIUM: 29MG; CARBOHYDRATES: 68G; FIBER: 18G; PROTEIN: 29G

Mango White Bean

Beans are an essential part of any weight management or diabetic meal plan. Beans provide slow-digesting carbohydrates for long lasting energy and stable blood sugar levels. A secret ingredient for smoothies, beans add creaminess, protein, vitamins, minerals, and fiber.

1 cup cashew milk
⅓ cup white beans, rinsed
½ cup frozen mango
½ cup frozen spinach (or 2 cups fresh)
2 tablespoons hemp seeds
1 tablespoon coconut flour
2 tablespoons chopped fresh mint leaves, for garnish
½ to 1 cup ice

Optional Add-Ins:

½ cup Greek yogurt
½ cup silken tofu
1 tablespoon chia seed gel
1 teaspoon coconut oil

Combine all of the ingredients and blend until smooth. Serve right away.

Serves 1 | Per Serving: CALORIES: 426; TOTAL FAT: 9G; SUGAR: 13G; SODIUM: 42MG; CARBOHYDRATES: 65G; FIBER: 17G; PROTEIN: 26G

low sugar

high protein

high fiber

Cashew milk is relatively new to grocery store shelves, so if you can't find it, substitute with unsweetened almond milk. For more protein, try soy milk or nonfat dairy milk.

**high
protein**

**high
fiber**

Powdered peanut butter is sold under several brand names, including PB2 and PBFit. Find it at your local grocer and big-box retailers.

Peanut Butter Raspberry

Reminiscent of a peanut butter and jelly flavor combination, research has shown that the phytochemical anthocyanin in cherries may help promote weight loss and reduce the risk of type 2 diabetes. Packed with protein and bursting with peanut flavor, enjoy a nutritious version of this classic favorite.

¾ cup nonfat milk, soy milk, or protein-fortified almond milk
½ cup silken tofu
¾ cup frozen cherries
2 tablespoons powdered peanut butter
1 tablespoon unsweetened peanut butter
1 tablespoon psyllium husk
½ to 1 cup ice

Optional Add-Ins:

½ frozen banana
1 tablespoon chopped peanuts, for garnish
1 tablespoon chia seed gel
1 teaspoon cinnamon

Combine all of the ingredients and blend until smooth. Serve right away.

Serves 1 | Per Serving: CALORIES: 424; TOTAL FAT: 16G; SUGAR: 22G; SODIUM: 299MG; CARBOHYDRATES: 68G; FIBER: 33G; PROTEIN: 20G

Apricot Cottage Cheese

This smoothie is high in slow-digesting protein from cottage cheese and complex carbs from rolled oats. Sweetness and nutrition are provided by apricots and raspberries, two fantastic fruits noted for their high-fiber, low-calorie content. A great recipe for a filling breakfast or hearty afternoon snack.

½ cup water
½ cup cottage cheese
2 chopped apricots
½ cup frozen raspberries
2 tablespoons rolled oats
2 tablespoons ground flaxseed
1 pitted and chopped Medjool date
½ teaspoon vanilla extract
pinch nutmeg
stevia (optional)
½ to 1 cup ice

Optional Add-Ins:
½ cup frozen spinach
1 tablespoon hemp seeds
1 teaspoon cinnamon

Combine all of the ingredients and blend until smooth. Serve right away.

Serves 1 | Per Serving: CALORIES: 489; TOTAL FAT: 9G; SUGAR: 51G; SODIUM: 465MG; CARBOHYDRATES: 80G; FIBER: 14G; PROTEIN: 23G

Apricot season in the United States runs from May through August. In winter, apricots are imported from South America. Buy them when they are in season and wash, pit, slice, and store them in your freezer.

Coconut flour is a low-carb thickener that adds fiber and a tropical taste. Substitute oat bran, almond flour, or chia gel for the same consistency.

Edamame Avocado

Avocado and edamame team up in this creamy, sweet smoothie. Shelled edamame, or green soybeans, are a complete protein, meaning they have all of the essential amino acids your body needs. A key part of any meal, protein provides satiety, keeps blood sugar steady, and is an essential weight-loss aid.

¾ cup nonfat milk, soy milk, or protein-fortified almond milk
½ cup shelled edamame
¼ cup avocado
½ cup frozen mango
1 tablespoon coconut flour
stevia (optional)
½ to 1 cup ice

Optional Add-Ins:

½ cup frozen spinach
1 tablespoon ground flaxseed
1 teaspoon coconut oil
shredded coconut, for garnish

Combine all of the ingredients and blend until smooth. Serve right away.

Serves 1 | Per Serving: CALORIES: 345; TOTAL FAT: 15G; SUGAR: 21G; SODIUM: 118MG; CARBOHYDRATES: 39G; FIBER: 10G; PROTEIN: 16G

Cocoa Craver

Chocolate lovers rejoice! The polyphenols in dark cocoa may help aid weight loss and fat metabolism. Not to be confused with chocolate, cocoa is the nonfat component that contains naturally occurring antioxidants without the sugar and fat. Rich and delicious, a healthful way to satisfy cravings.

½ cup water
6 ounces plain Greek yogurt
½ cup frozen strawberries
½ cup frozen kale (or 2 cups fresh)
¼ cup cooked quinoa
1 tablespoon unsweetened cocoa
1 tablespoon almond butter
1 tablespoon chia seeds
½ teaspoon vanilla extract
stevia (optional)
½ to 1 cup ice

Optional Add-Ins:

2 tablespoons avocado
1 tablespoon psyllium husk
1 teaspoon cinnamon
⅛ teaspoon cayenne

Combine all of the ingredients and blend until smooth. Serve right away.

Serves 1 | Per Serving: CALORIES: 483; TOTAL FAT: 24G; SUGAR: 16G; SODIUM: 173MG; CARBOHYDRATES: 54G; FIBER: 10G; PROTEIN: 20G

high
protein

Quinoa adds protein, fiber, and slow-digesting carbs. You can easily substitute rolled oats, leftover cooked brown rice, or oat bran for similar nutrition and texture.

You can substitute canned pumpkin for the sweet potato for similar nutrition and taste. Just choose 100% pumpkin and not pumpkin pie filling.

Sweet Potato Pie

If you only eat sweet potatoes when they are covered in marshmallows, you're missing out on one of nature's truly perfect foods. They're low in calories, high in fiber, great for diabetics, and packed with vitamins and minerals. Loaded with goodness, their sweet flavor is paired with orange and cinnamon for a delicious and filling pie in a glass.

½ cup unsweetened almond milk
6 ounces plain Greek yogurt
½ cup sweet potato, cooked and peeled
1 small orange, peeled
½ frozen banana
¼ cup rolled oats
1 tablespoon ground flaxseed
¼ teaspoon cinnamon (optional)
½ to 1 cup ice

Optional Add-Ins:
1 serving protein powder of your choice
1 tablespoon hemp seed
1 teaspoon vanilla extract
1 teaspoon nutmeg
1 small apple, peeled and cored

Combine all of the ingredients and blend until smooth. Serve right away.

Serves 1 | Per Serving: CALORIES: 499; TOTAL FAT: 16G; SUGAR: 38G; SODIUM: 232MG; CARBOHYDRATES: 77G; FIBER: 12G; PROTEIN: 15G

Slimming Greens and Herbs

With almost six servings of fruits and veggies, this slimming smoothie is rich in vitamins, minerals, and phytochemicals. Thanks to added protein from Greek yogurt and the fiber from the produce and added flax, this incredibly filling smoothie will keep you from reaching for that bagel or doughnut you didn't really want.

1 cup water
½ cup plain nonfat Greek yogurt
1 cup romaine lettuce, chopped
2 stalks celery, chopped
2 cups baby spinach
½ frozen banana
1 pear, cored and chopped
juice of ½ lemon
⅓ cup chopped fresh cilantro (can substitute parsley)
1 tablespoon ground flaxseed
½ to 1 cup ice

Optional Add-Ins:

1 serving of protein powder of your choice
1 tablespoon hemp seed
1 small apple, peeled and cored

Combine all of the ingredients and blend until smooth. Serve right away.

Serves 1 | Per Serving: CALORIES: 258; TOTAL FAT: 3G; SUGAR: 27G; SODIUM: 124MG; CARBOHYDRATES: 46G; FIBER: 10G; PROTEIN: 16G

high protein

veggie lover

green smoothie

low calorie

For an extra calorie-burning metabolism boost, replace the water with brewed and chilled green tea and add a dash of cayenne.

protein

high
fiber

You can substitute nonfat milk or soy milk for the protein-fortified almond milk. You could also use water and a serving of your favorite protein powder.

Tropical Kiwi Pineapple Protein

This sweet and creamy tropical-tasting smoothie can help you start your day feeling full, which means you will have an easier time making good food choices as the day goes on. High in protein, healthy fats, fiber, and vitamins and minerals, power up your blender with this delicious mix.

½ cup protein-fortified almond milk
1 cup nonfat vanilla Greek yogurt
1 cup fresh pineapple
1 medium kiwi, skin intact
2 tablespoons unsweetened coconut
6 almonds
1 tablespoon psyllium husk
1 tablespoon ground flaxseed
½ to 1 cup ice

Optional Add-Ins:

1 to 2 cups dark leafy greens
¼ cup white beans
1 tablespoon coconut flour

Combine all of the ingredients and blend until smooth. Serve right away.

Serves 1 | Per Serving: CALORIES: 537; TOTAL FAT: 11G; SUGAR: 55G; SODIUM: 281MG; CARBOHYDRATES: 105G; FIBER: 37G; PROTEIN: 24G

Green Tea and Vegetable Smoothie

Perfect for keeping blood sugar levels steady and your metabolism fired, this creamy smoothie uses green peas for added protein and fiber, and chia for healthy fats. In a base of weight loss–promoting, calcium-rich Greek yogurt, watching your waistline never tasted so good.

1 cup brewed and chilled green tea
¾ cup nonfat Greek yogurt
½ cup frozen broccoli
½ cup frozen cauliflower
⅓ cup frozen green peas
½ cup frozen mango
½ frozen banana
2 tablespoons chia seeds
stevia (optional)
½ to 1 cup ice

Optional Add-Ins:

1 tablespoon rice bran
¼ cup rolled oats
1 to 2 cups leafy greens

Combine all of the ingredients and blend until smooth. Serve right away.

Serves 1 | Per Serving: CALORIES: 322; TOTAL FAT: 6G; SUGAR: 37G; SODIUM: 168MG; CARBOHYDRATES: 61G; FIBER: 15G; PROTEIN: 18G

veggie lover

high protein

high fiber

If you don't have time to brew tea, replace with water and add 1 teaspoon powdered matcha for a more concentrated metabolism booster.

Digestion Support

Millions of people suffer every day from some form of digestive issues. We eat too fast, don't chew our food carefully, rush away from the table, or worse yet, choose foods high in fat and salt and low in fiber. Instead of turning to antacids or other drugs, be proactive by eating a wide variety of whole, unprocessed foods. Smoothies are a great way to include a number of digestion-supporting foods and herbs in your diet on a regular basis. Because they are blended drinks made with fresh ingredients, they allow you to get the vitamins, minerals, and fiber you need without overly taxing your digestive system. Digestion-friendly foods include hemp, chia, and flaxseed—filled with fiber; pectin-rich fruits like apples, pears, avocados, and bananas; and probiotic cultured products such as kefir, dairy yogurt, soy yogurt, and coconut yogurt. Other foods that help improve digestion are spices and herbs such as fennel, parsley, mint, and ginger. Have fun experimenting with the following recipes.

Cacao Beet

Kefir is a dairy drink similar to yogurt; it contains many enzymes, and has a tart taste. Kefir has beneficial bacteria that colonize the intestinal tract, instead of just feeding healthy bacteria like yogurt does. Rich in fiber and phytochemicals, ease your digestion with this nutritious drink.

½ cup almond milk
½ cup kefir
½ cup frozen cranberries
1 frozen banana
½ cup beets
1 tablespoon cacao or cocoa
2 tablespoons hemp seeds
1 to 2 pitted Medjool dates
½ to 1 cup ice

Optional Add-Ins:

Dash of cinnamon
1 teaspoon acacia powder
¼ cup avocado
1 tablespoon chia gel

Combine all of the ingredients and blend until smooth. Serve right away.

Serves 1 | Per Serving: CALORIES: 507; TOTAL FAT: 14G; SUGAR: 65G; SODIUM: 210MG; CARBOHYDRATES: 93G; FIBER: 14G; PROTEIN: 14G

high protein

For maximum flavor and nutrition, buy small fresh red beets and steam them unpeeled, with several inches of the tips left on. Remove the tops and slip the peels off while the beets are still warm.

protein

low
calorie

↘ If your grocer
doesn't carry plain kefir,
you can substitute with
plain acidophilus yogurt
(not regular yogurt) as
each contains beneficial
bacteria.

Digestion-Friendly Turmeric Lassi

Inspired by the traditional Indian beverage made with yogurt
and an assortment of herbs and spices, this drink is rich
in digestive enzymes, friendly bacteria, fiber, and the anti-
inflammatory power of turmeric. Serve with a sprinkle of
cardamom on top for extra warmth.

1 cup plain kefir
1 cup frozen papaya
2 teaspoons fresh ginger, grated
1 teaspoon turmeric
2 tablespoons ground flaxseed
1 teaspoon honey
juice of ½ lemon
½ to 1 cup ice

Optional Add-Ins:

½ frozen banana
¼ cup avocado
1 small pear, cored, peel on
1 tablespoon chia gel

Combine all of the ingredients and blend until smooth.
Serve right away.

Serves 1 | Per Serving: CALORIES: 298; TOTAL FAT: 8G; SUGAR: 25G;
SODIUM: 143MG; CARBOHYDRATES: 41G; FIBER: 10G; PROTEIN: 18G

Pineapple Parsley Mint

This electrolyte rich green smoothie is packed with digestion-enhancing and immune-boosting foods including pineapple, parsley, mint, ginger, and avocado. Easy on the stomach, this makes a great breakfast or afternoon snack. Serve with a slice of lemon.

½ cup water
½ cup coconut water
1 cup frozen pineapple chunks
½ frozen banana
2 tablespoons hemp seeds
2 tablespoons avocado
¼ cup packed fresh parsley
¼ cup packed fresh mint
1 teaspoon freshly grated ginger
½ to 1 cup ice

Optional Add-Ins:

¼ teaspoon probiotic powder
2 cups dark leafy greens
1 teaspoon honey
1 tablespoon chia gel

Combine all of the ingredients and blend until smooth. Serve right away.

Serves 1 | Per Serving: CALORIES: 455; TOTAL FAT: 13G; SUGAR: 64G; SODIUM: 96MG; CARBOHYDRATES: 75G; FIBER: 8G; PROTEIN: 10G

high protein

For more probiotic power, substitute soy yogurt for the water. Kefir and dairy yogurt may curdle from the citric acid in the pineapple.

The gel that chia seeds form when they sit in water is what makes this food a "demulcent," a food that coats and soothes your stomach. Combine 1 part chia seeds to 1 part water and let it sit for 15 to 20 minutes.

Avocado Banana Soothing Smoothie

This creamy smoothie is sure to soothe and calm a distressed digestive system. Avocados are rich in healthy fats and fiber, and bananas contain pectin and stimulate the growth of friendly bacteria. In a base of probiotic rich kefir and yogurt, this is so yummy you'll forget how healthy it is.

½ cup plain kefir
½ cup plain Greek yogurt
½ cup avocado, chopped
1 frozen banana, sliced
2 tablespoons chia seed gel
1 teaspoon vanilla extract
2 teaspoons honey
½ to 1 cup ice

Optional Add-Ins:

1 small apple, peeled, cored, and cubed
Dash of cinnamon
2 tablespoons hemp seeds

Combine all of the ingredients and blend until smooth. Serve right away.

Serves 1 | Per Serving: CALORIES: 450; TOTAL FAT: 17G; SUGAR: 34G; SODIUM: 116MG; CARBOHYDRATES: 56G; FIBER: 11G; PROTEIN: 22G

Pear Ginger Digestion Booster

A well-running digestive tract can have an amazing effect on energy levels. Adequate fiber, healthy fats, and extra GI (gastrointestinal) boosters like ginger and lemon are some of the best ways to enhance your digestion. This healing smoothie gets its creamy texture from pectin-rich pears and creamy avocado.

1 cup plain soy yogurt
1 large pear, cored and chopped
1 stalk celery
1 tablespoon grated fresh ginger
¼ cup avocado
2 cups baby spinach
1 tablespoon ground flaxseed
1 teaspoon lemon juice
1 teaspoon honey
½ to 1 cup ice

Optional Add-Ins:

½ frozen banana
1 tablespoon chia gel
3 to 4 fresh mint leaves
¼ teaspoon probiotic powder

Combine all of the ingredients and blend until smooth.
Serve right away.

Serves 1 | Per Serving: CALORIES: 440; TOTAL FAT: 16G; SUGAR: 37G; SODIUM: 90MG; CARBOHYDRATES: 64G; FIBER: 13G; PROTEIN: 15G

green smoothie

high protein

↘ You can substitute any type of cultured yogurt for the soy yogurt. For maximum probiotic power look for brands that include *L. acidophilus, S. thermophilus, L. bulgaricus, bifidus* and *L. casei* on their ingredient lists.

low calorie

high fiber

Herbs are easy to freeze and ensure you always have some on hand. Simply rinse, chop, place in ice cube trays, cover with water, and freeze.

Watermelon Digester

Probiotic-rich coconut yogurt serves as the base in this hydrating, refreshing smoothie. More than just water and sugar, watermelon is high in fiber and phytochemicals, and sweet pineapple contains the digestive enzyme bromelain. With a dash of mint, this refreshing smoothie can keep your GI system humming along.

1 cup plain coconut yogurt
1 cup watermelon chunks
½ cup frozen pineapple
2 tablespoons ground flaxseed
2 tablespoons chopped fresh mint leaves
½ teaspoon cinnamon
1 teaspoon honey
½ to 1 cup ice

Optional Add-Ins:

½ frozen banana
½ cup frozen berries
1 tablespoon hemp seeds
1 tablespoon chia gel

Combine all of the ingredients and blend until smooth. Serve right away.

Serves 1 | Per Serving: CALORIES: 296; TOTAL FAT: 13G; SUGAR: 33G; SODIUM: 203MG; CARBOHYDRATES: 50G; FIBER: 16G; PROTEIN: 4G

Herbed Pineapple Green Apple

high protein

Each ingredient in this creamy, flavorful smoothie has stomach-soothing properties to calm your digestive tract. Hemp seeds and honey act as demulcents to soothe and coat, pectin-rich apple adds soluble fiber, and pineapple adds digestive enzymes. Finished with an herbal trifecta, enjoy this stomach soother.

½ cup water
½ cup plain soy yogurt
½ cup frozen pineapple chunks
1 green apple, cored and chopped
1 tablespoon fresh fennel bulb, chopped
3 to 4 fresh mint leaves
1 tablespoon fresh ginger, chopped
juice of 1 small lemon
2 tablespoons hemp seeds
1 teaspoon honey
½ to 1 cup ice

Optional Add-Ins:

1 tablespoon chia gel
1 cup chopped celery
1 to 2 cups dark leafy greens
½ frozen banana

Combine all of the ingredients and blend until smooth.
Serve right away.

Substitute lightly ground fennel or anise seeds for fresh fennel. If you are feeling adventurous, steam fresh artichoke hearts for a boost of digestion-friendly prebiotics.

Serves 1 | Per Serving: CALORIES: 440; TOTAL FAT: 11G; SUGAR: 59G; SODIUM: 32MG; CARBOHYDRATES: 80G; FIBER: 11G; PROTEIN: 13G

protein

high
fiber

To make this into a complete meal and increase the protein content, add one or more of the optional add-ins.

Blackberry Stomach Support

Get a jump-start on your recommended fiber intake for the day with this scrumptious, creamy smoothie made from phytochemical-, vitamin-, mineral-, and fiber-rich blackberries. Sweetened by bananas and pears and with a probiotic protein punch from Greek yogurt, this makes a great breakfast.

½ cup almond milk
½ cup plain Greek yogurt
1 cup frozen blackberries
½ frozen banana
1 small pear, cored and chopped
¼ cup chopped avocado
1 teaspoon grated fresh ginger
1 pitted Medjool date
½ to 1 cup ice

Optional Add-Ins:

1 tablespoon chia gel
2 tablespoons ground wheat germ
2 tablespoons rolled oats
2 tablespoons hemp seeds

Combine all of the ingredients and blend until smooth. Serve right away.

Serves 1 | Per Serving: CALORIES: 437; TOTAL FAT: 10G; SUGAR: 52G; SODIUM: 134MG; CARBOHYDRATES: 79G; FIBER: 18G; PROTEIN: 16G

Strawberry Kefir Stomach Soother

This sweet, earthy-tasting smoothie is loaded with probiotics, vitamin C, fiber, vitamins, and minerals. As nutritious as it is creamy and delicious, add this to your morning routine and it will prime your body for better and easier digestion all day long.

1 cup plain kefir
½ cup frozen strawberries
½ frozen banana
½ cup steamed and peeled red beets, cubed
¼ cup rolled oats
2 tablespoons ground flaxseed
1 Medjool date
½ to 1 cup ice

Optional Add-Ins:

2 cups dark leafy greens
1 teaspoon cinnamon
1 teaspoon grated fresh ginger

Combine all of the ingredients and blend until smooth. Serve right away.

Serves 1 | Per Serving: CALORIES: 452; TOTAL FAT: 9G; SUGAR: 43G; SODIUM: 196MG; CARBOHYDRATES: 75G; FIBER: 15G; PROTEIN: 22G

high protein

high fiber

Golden or yellow beets tend to be sweeter and taste a little less earthy and more mellow in intensity than red beets. Golden beets are also packed with nutrients, so eat up!

You can use any type of melon in this recipe: cantaloupe, honeydew, musk melon, or crenshaw. Seasonal produce has the highest nutritional content.

Fennel Melon Digestive Ease

Easy on the digestive system, melon and cucumber team up with a backup crew of potent digestion support herbs to deliver a one-two punch of stomach calm. With a unique flavor and creamy consistency, enjoy the detoxifying powers of this nutrient-rich smoothie.

1 cup plain soy yogurt
½ cup fresh melon, chopped
½ cup chopped cucumber
½ frozen banana
2 tablespoons hemp seeds
¼ cup chopped fennel bulb
3 to 4 fresh mint leaves
½ to 1 cup ice

Optional Add-Ins:

1 tablespoon grated fresh ginger
1 tablespoon ground flaxseed
1 to 2 pitted Medjool dates
1 tablespoon chopped fresh parsley

Combine all of the ingredients and blend until smooth. Serve right away.

Serves 1 | Per Serving: CALORIES: 387; TOTAL FAT: 14G; SUGAR: 31G; SODIUM: 59MG; CARBOHYDRATES: 53G; FIBER: 9G; PROTEIN: 18G

Cantaloupe Kefir

This creamy and hydrating smoothie is teeming with probiotics, fiber, and friendly flora to support a healthy digestive system. Cantaloupe is high in folic acid, vitamins A and C, potassium, and fiber. It also helps promote regularity and its sweet taste blends beautifully with creamy banana for a refreshing breakfast or afternoon snack.

1 cup plain kefir
½ cup plain Greek yogurt
1½ cups diced ripe cantaloupe
½ frozen banana
1 tablespoon chia seeds
½ teaspoon vanilla extract
½ to 1 cup ice

Optional Add-Ins:

1 teaspoon honey
1 tablespoon ground flaxseed
¼ teaspoon probiotic power

Combine all of the ingredients and blend until smooth. Serve right away.

Serves 1 | Per Serving: CALORIES: 352; TOTAL FAT: 6G; SUGAR: 38G; SODIUM: 211MG; CARBOHYDRATES: 51G; FIBER: 9G; PROTEIN: 30G

high protein

↘ Choose deep-orange cantaloupes for the best flavor, but if you find your melon isn't sweet enough, simply add a dash of honey, stevia, or a pitted Medjool date.

Spicy Banana Apple

The typical BRAT (bananas, brown rice, applesauce, toast) diet for belly upsets calls for brown rice, which you can substitute for the oats in this recipe.

This simple yet nutritious, creamy, and delicious smoothie includes foods known to promote healthy digestion and calm common upsets such as indigestion and nausea. More than just a sweet creamy ingredient for smoothies, bananas are easy to digest and are full or prebiotics that feed your gut bacteria. Enjoy this regularly as part of a healthy eating plan.

½ cup unsweetened almond milk
½ cup plain acidophilus yogurt
1 medium frozen banana, sliced
1 apple, peeled and cored
¼ cup rolled oats
½ teaspoon grated fresh ginger
½ teaspoon ground cinnamon
½ teaspoon vanilla extract
½ to 1 cup ice

Optional Add-Ins:

1 tablespoon chia seed gel
2 tablespoons unsweetened applesauce
1 to 2 pitted Medjool dates
¼ teaspoon coriander or cardamom

Combine all of the ingredients and blend until smooth. Serve right away.

Serves 1 | Per Serving: CALORIES: 384; TOTAL FAT: 8G; SUGAR: 40G; SODIUM: 151MG; CARBOHYDRATES: 75G; FIBER: 11G; PROTEIN: 9G

Calming Peach Chamomile

Chamomile tea has been traditionally used in herbal medicine to help relieve mild digestive disturbances as well as to help calm nerves and promote restful sleep, and it is used as the liquid in this tummy-taming smoothie. Enjoy this after a strenuous workout or a stressful day.

1 cup brewed and chilled chamomile tea
½ cup plain acidophilus yogurt
1 cup frozen peaches
¼ cup rolled oats
1 tablespoon ground flaxseed
½ teaspoon grated fresh ginger
1 teaspoon honey
½ to 1 cup ice

Optional Add-Ins:
1 tablespoon dried chamomile
1 teaspoon vanilla extract
1 tablespoon chia seed gel

Combine all of the ingredients and blend until smooth. Serve right away.

Serves 1 | Per Serving: CALORIES: 292; TOTAL FAT: 6G; SUGAR: 29G; SODIUM: 90MG; CARBOHYDRATES: 47G; FIBER: 7G; PROTEIN: 13G

high protein

low calorie

For a variation, heat 2 chamomile tea bags in almond milk in the microwave or stop top, let steep for 10 minutes, then chill for an hour before using as the liquid base.

Brain and Energy Boosters

If you feel fatigued most of the time, you are not alone. Before you turn to sugary highly caffeinated energy drinks, consider your diet. With the right ingredients, your morning smoothie can give you the energy, concentration, and focus you need to power your day and add to your overall nutrition and health. Energizing smoothies should have protein and healthy fats for satiety, high-fiber carbs for slow-burning energy, and targeted ingredients that can help improve focus, concentration, and memory without the use of refined sugars and artificial ingredients. Foods like broccoli and wheat germ are rich in choline, a B vitamin important for neurotransmitter function, while peanuts and spinach are rich in CoQ_{10}, a nutrient that is important for producing energy. Use the recipes in this chapter and the Mix-and-Match charts in Chapter 1 to develop your personal favorite smoothies for natural energy that will last all day long.

Morning Matcha

Matcha or "powdered tea" is made from the leaves of green tea, making it a potent source of antioxidants and the metabolism-boosting polyphenol EGCG. Matcha is also high in L-theanine, which promotes concentration and focus. Paired with slow-burning carbs and healthy fats, this drink will supercharge your day.

¾ cup unsweetened almond milk
½ cup Greek yogurt
½ frozen banana
½ cup frozen spinach
¼ cup rolled oats
¼ cup almonds
2 teaspoons matcha powder
2 teaspoons honey
½ to 1 cup ice

Optional Add-Ins:

¼ cup frozen berries
1 tablespoon ground flaxseed
1 tablespoon maca powder

Combine all of the ingredients and blend until smooth. Serve right away.

Serves 1 | Per Serving: CALORIES: 533; TOTAL FAT: 20G; SUGAR: 30G; SODIUM: 374MG; CARBOHYDRATES: 64G; FIBER: 12G; PROTEIN: 30G

meal swap

high protein

If you don't have matcha powder on hand, brew a cup of strong green tea, chill in the fridge, and use in place of the almond milk.

veggie
lover

high
protein

↘ For a sweeter taste and more vitamin C, replace the soy milk with orange juice, and add a dash of lime juice and agave syrup (optional).

Beet Raspberry Kale

Naturally sweet, beets are filled with vitamins and minerals. Here they are paired with iron-rich kale and slow-digesting protein to give you long-lasting energy. An amazingly refreshing drink, the addition of ginger helps improve circulation, giving you a natural energy boost.

½ cup soy milk
½ cup silken tofu
1 large beet, cooked, peeled and diced (about 1 cup)
juice of 1 orange
1 tablespoon chia seeds
½ cup frozen raspberries
½ cup frozen kale
1-inch piece ginger
stevia (optional)
½ to 1 cup ice

Optional Add-Ins:

½ cup frozen spinach
1 tablespoon ground flaxseed
1 teaspoon vanilla extract
1 teaspoon cinnamon

Combine all of the ingredients and blend until smooth. Serve right away.

Serves 1 | Per Serving: CALORIES: 385; TOTAL FAT: 8G; SUGAR: 47G; SODIUM: 181MG; CARBOHYDRATES: 69G; FIBER: 13G; PROTEIN: 16G

Berry Brain Booster

Boost your brain power with this smoothie packed with foods that are good for the mind. Broccoli contributes the B vitamin choline, known for its role in memory and learning. Blueberries and hemp seeds provide antioxidants and omega-3 fats to keep your brain cells healthy. Kick it up a notch with one or more brain-boosting add-ins.

½ cup apple juice
½ cup Greek yogurt
1 cup frozen blueberries
½ cup frozen broccoli
2 tablespoons hemp seeds
1 tablespoon wheat germ
½ to 1 cup ice

Optional Add-Ins:

1 tablespoon walnuts
1 teaspoon coconut oil
½ cup chopped celery
⅛ teaspoon tumeric

Combine all of the ingredients and blend until smooth. Serve right away.

Serves 1 | Per Serving: CALORIES: 333; TOTAL FAT: 8G; SUGAR: 38G; SODIUM: 110MG; CARBOHYDRATES: 54G; FIBER: 8G; PROTEIN: 16G

high protein

Add ¼ cup chopped avocado to make your smoothie creamier and to boost the content of monounsaturated fat, a type of fat that can keep brain cell membranes flexible.

Dates add a rich flavor and provide sweetness, but if you find them expensive, substitute the sweetener of your choice and add 1 tablespoon chia for a similar consistency.

Cacao Oatmeal

Our concentration skills are linked to the brain's supply of glucose, so you want to fuel up with foods that supply steady energy. Whole-grain oats, soy milk, and fiber-rich pumpkin fit the bill as healthy brain foods to keep you fueled and energized. Cocoa, a nutrient shown to improve blood flow to the brain, adds a delicious and nutritious touch.

1 cup soy milk
½ cup canned pumpkin
⅓ cup rolled oats
2 tablespoons almonds
1 tablespoon unsweetened cacao or cocoa
1 to 2 pitted Medjool dates
½ to 1 cup ice

Optional Add-Ins:

2 tablespoons cacao nibs
2 tablespoons powdered peanut butter
½ cup frozen peaches

Combine all of the ingredients and blend until smooth. Serve right away.

Serves 1 | Per Serving: CALORIES: 490; TOTAL FAT: 13G; SUGAR: 47G; SODIUM: 134MG; CARBOHYDRATES: 85G; FIBER: 14G; PROTEIN: 17G

Strawberry Spinach Kickstarter

CoQ_{10} is an antioxidant made by the body that helps produce energy, neutralize free radicals, and may even improve athletic performance. You can boost your intake naturally with this CoQ_{10}-rich smoothie made with some of the best food sources of this nutrient.

1 cup unsweetened almond milk
½ cup frozen strawberries
½ cup frozen spinach
1 tablespoon peanut butter
2 tablespoons sesame seeds
1 to 2 pitted Medjool dates
½ to 1 cup ice

Optional Add-Ins:

1 tablespoon pistachios
1 medium orange
½ cup frozen broccoli

Combine all of the ingredients and blend until smooth. Serve right away.

Serves 1 | Per Serving: CALORIES: 398; TOTAL FAT: 21G; SUGAR: X38; SODIUM: 267MG; CARBOHYDRATES: 52G; FIBER: 9G; PROTEIN: 10G

veggie lover

high protein

Rice bran is a natural source of CoQ_{10} and has a creamy vanilla flavor that is perfect for smoothies. Find it in the baking or hot cereal aisle of your local grocery store.

sugar

low
calorie

↘ Coconut milk is different from coconut water. Coconut milk is found canned and contains significant amounts of fat in the form of beneficial medium-chain triglycerides. Add ¼ cup for extra creaminess and nutrition.

Papaya Maca Invigorator

One possible cause for fatigue is simply dehydration, which is one of the reasons smoothies are so energizing. This recipe features coconut water, which is an excellent source of potassium, an important electrolyte involved in fluid balance. Maca, a superfood noted for its ability to increase stamina and boost energy, is a perfect complement to this smoothie, adding an earthy taste and nutty flavor.

1 cup coconut water
¼ cup chopped avocado
½ cup frozen papaya
½ cup frozen kale
2 tablespoons sunflower seeds
1 teaspoon maca powder
½ to 1 cup ice

Optional Add-Ins:

¼ cup coconut milk
½ cup Greek yogurt or silken tofu
1 teaspoon coconut oil
1 teaspoon wheatgrass powder

Combine all of the ingredients and blend until smooth. Serve right away.

Serves 1 | Per Serving: CALORIES: 178; TOTAL FAT: 10G; SUGAR: 7G; SODIUM: 16MG; CARBOHYDRATES: 19G; FIBER: 7G; PROTEIN: 5G

Peach Quinoa Plant Pep

This smoothie is powered by high-quality plant protein from three complete protein sources: quinoa, soy yogurt, and hemp seeds. Providing a steady stream of energy, this sweet and nourishing drink gives your brain and body antioxidants and omega-3 fats for clean, healthy fuel.

½ cup water
6 ounces plain soy yogurt
½ cup frozen peaches
½ cup frozen spinach
¼ cup cooked quinoa
2 tablespoons hemp seeds
1 to 2 pitted Medjool dates
½ to 1 cup ice

Optional Add-Ins:
2 tablespoons powdered peanut butter
¼ cup shelled edamame
1 tablespoon almond butter

Combine all of the ingredients and blend until smooth. Serve right away.

Serves 1 | Per Serving: CALORIES: 474; TOTAL FAT: 13G; SUGAR: 52G; SODIUM: 28MG; CARBOHYDRATES: 78G; FIBER: 8G; PROTEIN: 18G

Cook grains in bulk on the weekends and portion out and refrigerate or freeze the amount you need for your weekly smoothies. Choosing your recipes and doing prep in advance is a great time-saver for busy mornings.

meal
swap

low
sugar

high
protein

Replace the almond milk with green tea for additional antioxidants, caffeine for alertness, and EGCG to boost metabolism, and finish with a splash of lemon juice and honey.

Blackberry Broccoli Pumpkin Seed

Bursting with brain-boosting superfoods: blackberries and broccoli provide vitamins C and K for mental agility, and pumpkin seeds add zinc for memory and thinking. Satiety is provided by high-protein cottage cheese, and whole-grain oats provide a steady supply of energy for your brain.

¾ cup unsweetened almond milk
½ cup cottage cheese
1 cup frozen blackberries
½ cup frozen broccoli
¼ cup pumpkin seeds
¼ cup rolled oats
stevia (optional)
½ to 1 cup ice

Optional Add-Ins:

½ cup frozen spinach
½ frozen banana
1 tablespoon chia seeds

Combine all of the ingredients and blend until smooth. Serve right away.

Serves 1 | Per Serving: CALORIES: 473; TOTAL FAT: 23G; SUGAR: 9G; SODIUM: 618MG; CARBOHYDRATES: 42G; FIBER: 13G; PROTEIN: 31G

Strawberry Sunrise

Pomegranate juice gives this smoothie a splash of color and a unique pleasant taste. The antioxidants in pomegranate juice may improve blood flow, especially to the heart and brain, making this fruit juice an excellent liquid base for natural energy and nutrition.

½ cup pomegranate juice
½ cup Greek yogurt
¾ cup frozen strawberries
2 tablespoons ground flaxseed
2 tablespoons chopped avocado
½ to 1 cup ice

Optional Add-Ins:

2 tablespoons goji berries
½ cup frozen kale
1 tablespoon hemp seeds

Combine all of the ingredients and blend until smooth. Serve right away.

Serves 1 | Per Serving: CALORIES: 299; TOTAL FAT: 10G; SUGAR: 27G; SODIUM: 43MG; CARBOHYDRATES: 38G; FIBER: 7G; PROTEIN: 13G

high protein

low calorie

↘ If pomegranate juice doesn't fit your budget, swap it out for 100% cranberry, blueberry, or cherry juice, all excellent sources of antioxidants and phytochemicals.

meal
swap

high
protein

high
fiber

Protein powders vary widely in quality, price, and the texture they add to smoothies. Consider buying a few single-serving packets before investing in a large container.

Java Delight

Supercharge your brain with this smoothie containing foods that will help your body produce more dopamine, a neurotransmitter that carries nerve impulses to the brain. Bananas, soy, and nuts all supply the precursors while garbanzo beans add magnesium, a mineral that promotes blood flow to the brain.

¾ cup soy milk
¼ cup brewed and chilled strong coffee
1 frozen banana
¼ cup garbanzo beans
2 tablespoons walnuts
½ teaspoon ground cinnamon
½ teaspoon vanilla extract
1 serving vanilla protein powder
½ to 1 cup ice

Optional Add-Ins:
½ cup frozen blueberries
½ cup Greek yogurt
1 teaspoon spirulina
2 tablespoons avocado

Combine all of the ingredients and blend until smooth. Serve right away.

Serves 1 | Per Serving: CALORIES: 603; TOTAL FAT: 16G; SUGAR: 28G; SODIUM: 162MG; CARBOHYDRATES: 72G; FIBER: 15G; PROTEIN: 48G

Cherry Supercharger

The secret to making smoothies that give you energy is to use high quality, nutrient-dense ingredients, and go for a balance of protein, fiber, and healthy fats. This smoothie does just that by using a base of protein-rich tofu, nutrient-rich cherry juice, fruits, and beets that will give you a delicious and natural pick-me-up.

½ cup 100% tart cherry juice
½ cup silken tofu
½ cup frozen cherries
½ cup frozen cranberries
⅓ cup raw or roasted beets, diced
½ frozen banana
2 tablespoons hemp seeds
1 tablespoon wheat germ
1 teaspoon grated ginger
stevia (optional)
½ to 1 cup ice

Optional Add-Ins:

¼ avocado
1 apple, cored and sliced
1 to 2 cups dark leafy greens
1 teaspoon maca powder

Combine all of the ingredients and blend until smooth.
Serve right away.

Serves 1 | Per Serving: CALORIES: 430; TOTAL FAT: 11G; SUGAR: 48G; SODIUM: 196MG; CARBOHYDRATES: 71G; FIBER: 11G; PROTEIN: 18G

high
protein

superfood
star

Other nutrient-rich juices you could use are pomegranate and cranberry. You can also vary the berries depending on your personal preferences.

You can use any type of bean in this recipe: garbanzo, adzuki, black bean, kidney, and so on. If you are using canned, rinse your beans in a colander to remove excess sodium.

Chocolate Cocoa Pinto Bean

Skip the sugar-laden, high-calorie, high-priced fancy coffee drink and get your A game on with this power-packed smoothie instead. With just a touch of phytochemical-rich coffee for added focus, this protein- and fiber-rich smoothie is great for extra stamina.

½ cup unsweetened vanilla almond milk
½ cup Greek yogurt
½ cup frozen blueberries
½ frozen banana
2 tablespoons chopped avocado
½ cup pinto beans
1 pitted date, chopped
1 tablespoon unsweetened cacao
1 tablespoon chia seeds
1 teaspoon instant coffee
1 teaspoon vanilla extract
½ to 1 cup ice

Optional Add-Ins:
1 tablespoon wheat germ
1 to 2 cups dark leafy greens
1 tablespoon ground flaxseed

Combine all of the ingredients and blend until smooth. Serve right away.

Serves 1 | Per Serving: CALORIES: 425; TOTAL FAT: 11G; SUGAR: 25G; SODIUM: 330MG; CARBOHYDRATES: 66G; FIBER: 18G; PROTEIN: 22G

Goji Berry Chard Stabilizer

high protein

Erratic blood sugar levels have you down? Then try this smoothie high in slow-burning energy nutrients. Swiss chard is rich in vitamins and minerals and is unique in that it contains a flavonoid that has been shown to keep blood sugar levels steady. Goji berries add key phytochemicals and antioxidants. Soy milk and cottage cheese add protein for staying power.

½ cup plain soy milk
½ cup cottage cheese
2 cups Swiss chard, chopped, stems discarded
½ cup frozen strawberries
½ cup pineapple
2 tablespoons cashews
1 tablespoon ground flaxseed
1 tablespoon goji berries
½ to 1 cup ice

Optional Add-Ins:

2 tablespoons avocado
1 to 2 pitted Medjool dates
¼ cup rolled oats

Combine all of the ingredients and blend until smooth.
Serve right away.

Dried goji berries can be found in health food stores and larger grocery chains. If you have a hard time finding them, pomegranate seeds, or dried cranberries, cherries, or blueberries make delicious substitutions.

Serves 1 | Per Serving: CALORIES: 404; TOTAL FAT: 15G; SUGAR: 23G; SODIUM: 681MG; CARBOHYDRATES: 44G; FIBER: 8G; PROTEIN: 25G

Immune Support

A healthy diet is a necessity for a properly functioning immune system, and one of the easiest ways to ensure you are giving your body the nutrients it needs is to fill your diet with a mountainous, colorful array of fruits, vegetables, clean and lean proteins, unrefined grains, and healthy fats. A few tips to enhance your immunity like a pro are: avoid processed foods, drink plenty of water, get adequate exercise and rest, take time to relax, and include specific immune-enhancing nutrients in your diet, including probiotics, vitamins A, C, B_6, E, the minerals selenium and zinc, and a variety of phytochemicals. Making a smoothie is an easy, inexpensive, and delicious way to drink the vitamins, minerals, antioxidants, phytochemicals, and fiber you need to help keep you from getting sick. This practice also reduces your risk for chronic diseases like cancer. Enjoy the following recipes. Use the optional add-ins and substitution tips to customize the recipes to meet your particular health needs.

Immune Supporting Mango Ginger

Give your immune system a boost with this smoothie chock-full of phytochemicals, vitamin C, and potassium-rich vegetables and fruit. More than decoration on your plate, parsley's volatile oils contain powerful components for neutralizing free radicals. With a spicy kick from ginger, this smoothie is wonderfully nutritious.

1 cup coconut water
1 cup celery, chopped
1 cup parsley, fresh
1 cucumber, peeled and chopped
1 cup frozen mango
2 cups baby kale
1 tablespoon grated fresh ginger
juice of 1 lemon
½ to 1 cup ice

Optional Add-Ins:

½ frozen banana
½ cup silken tofu
pinch cayenne
½ avocado

Combine all of the ingredients and blend until smooth. Serve right away.

Serves 1 | Per Serving: CALORIES: 296; TOTAL FAT: 1G; SUGAR: 39G; SODIUM: 340MG; CARBOHYDRATES: 61G; FIBER: 11G; PROTEIN: 10G

green smoothie

veggie lover

high protein

Replace the coconut water with your favorite immune-boosting tea. White tea, green tea, rooibos, pu-erh, black, and oolong each have distinctive tastes for flavor variations.

protein

↘ Substitute 1 cup
loosely packed sweet
potato puree (about
1 large potato) for the
pumpkin. Bake at 400°F
for about 25 to 30 minutes
and let cool before adding
to the blender.

Pumpkin Orange Immune Booster

I buy organic canned pumpkin by the case—I adore it. It goes perfect in oats and gives a creamy consistency to smoothies. You can't go wrong with the exceptional nutrient content, as they are high in vitamins A and C, beta-carotene, and fiber. Enjoy this seriously delicious smoothie complimented by the spicy, warm undertones of anti-inflammatory spices.

¾ cup unsweetened almond milk
¼ cup orange juice
½ cup pumpkin puree (not pumpkin pie mix)
1 frozen banana, sliced
1 tablespoon almond butter
1 tablespoon ground flaxseed
¼ teaspoon ground turmeric
¼ teaspoon ground cinnamon
¼ teaspoon ground ginger (or 1 teaspoon fresh)
1 pitted Medjool date
½ to 1 cup ice

Optional Add-Ins:
½ cup soy yogurt
½ cup silken tofu
1 tablespoon wheat germ

Combine all of the ingredients and blend until smooth. Serve right away.

Serves 1 | Per Serving: CALORIES: 423; TOTAL FAT: 15G; SUGAR: 40G; SODIUM: 149MG; CARBOHYDRATES: 70G; FIBER: 12G; PROTEIN: 10G

Pomegranate Reboot

This smoothie is perfect for those days when you feel like your body could use a power boost from phytochemicals, antioxidants, and vitamin C. Rich in probiotics, vitamins C and E, fiber, and healthy fats, blend this up when you need some extra nutritional support.

½ cup pomegranate juice
½ cup Greek yogurt
⅓ cup frozen strawberries
⅓ cup frozen blackberries
¼ cup seedless grapes (red or green)
1 kiwi, cut into 4 pieces
⅓ cup papaya (cut into ½-inch pieces)
½ tablespoon flax oil
2 tablespoons wheat germ
½ to 1 cup ice

Optional Add-Ins:

¼ cup avocado
1 to 2 cups dark leafy greens
2 tablespoons chia seeds

Combine all of the ingredients and blend until smooth.
Serve right away.

Serves 1 | Per Serving: CALORIES: 534; TOTAL FAT: 13G; SUGAR: 61G; SODIUM: 83MG; CARBOHYDRATES: 81G; FIBER: 9G; PROTEIN: 26G

high protein

For lower sugar, replace the pomegranate juice with antioxidant-rich rooibos tea, or for added creaminess try almond, cashew, soy, or hemp milk—all rich in vitamin D.

protein

high
fiber

For added creaminess and to increase the zinc, protein, and fiber content, soak ¼ cup oats in the kefir overnight in the refrigerator and add to your smoothie.

Peanut Butter Immune Builder

There are hundreds of species of bacteria in your gut to help digest your food, and new evidence shows that a healthy gut is a key to a healthy immune system. With an added boost of vitamins C, B_6, D, and zinc, this sweet and creamy smoothie can support a healthy body.

1 cup kefir
½ cup soy yogurt
1 cup frozen strawberries
½ frozen banana
2 tablespoons peanut butter
1 tablespoon chia seeds
1 tablespoon wheat germ
1 pitted Medjool date
½ to 1 cup ice

Optional Add-Ins:
1 tablespoon ground flaxseed
¼ cup avocado
¼ teaspoon ground cinnamon
¼ cup rolled oats

Combine all of the ingredients and blend until smooth. Serve right away.

Serves 1 | Per Serving: CALORIES: 673; TOTAL FAT: 31G; SUGAR: 55G; SODIUM: 288MG; CARBOHYDRATES: 85G; FIBER: 16G; PROTEIN: 26G

Coconut Peach Power

This delicious smoothie makes it easy to keep viruses and colds at bay. Coconut oil contains lauric acid, an antiviral compound, and it adds extra richness to the sweet taste of creamy peaches. With added zinc and vitamins A and C from cashews, oats, and greens, this smoothie will make you feel your best.

1 cup coconut water
½ cup silken tofu
2 cups dark leafy greens (or ½ cup frozen)
1 cup frozen peaches
¼ cup cashews
¼ cup rolled oats
1 teaspoon coconut oil
1 pitted Medjool date
½ to 1 cup ice

Optional Add-Ins:

¼ teaspoon probiotic powder
1 teaspoon grated fresh ginger
1 tablespoon grated coconut

Combine all of the ingredients and blend until smooth. Serve right away.

Serves 1 | Per Serving: CALORIES: 546; TOTAL FAT: G;25 SUGAR: 42G; SODIUM: 244MG; CARBOHYDRATES: 63G; FIBER: 9G; PROTEIN: 17G

high
protein

↘ Substitute light canned coconut milk (not regular, which has far too much fat) for added creaminess and additional lauric acid, one of the medium-chain triglycerides in coconut.

protein

high
fiber

↘ Most beans are high in zinc as well as vitamin B$_6$, which is also important for immune health. If you feel like living on the edge, substitute garbanzos with green peas, which are an excellent source.

Raspberry Zinc Zinger

Zinc is a mineral that is important for immune function, and ensuring you get enough in your diet is one way to keep you healthy all year long. Raspberries, pumpkins seeds, garbanzo beans, avocado, and cacao all contain zinc. Too much zinc in supplement form can inhibit absorption of other minerals, so instead of popping some pills, pop this delicious mix in your blender.

½ cup unsweetened almond milk
½ cup Greek yogurt or soy yogurt
1 cup frozen raspberries
2 tablespoons avocado
2 tablespoons pumpkin seeds
¼ cup garbanzo beans
1 tablespoon unsweetened cacao or cocoa
2 pitted Medjool dates
½ to 1 cup ice

Optional Add-Ins:

1 tablespoon wheat germ
½ cup pomegranate seeds
1 to 2 cups dark leafy greens

Combine all of the ingredients and blend until smooth. Serve right away.

Serves 1 | Per Serving: CALORIES: 708; TOTAL FAT: 18G; SUGAR: 88G; SODIUM: 146MG; CARBOHYDRATES: 124G; FIBER: 20G; PROTEIN: 23G

Blueberry Kombucha

Kombucha is an ancient fermented tea-based probiotic beverage containing beneficial bacteria for digestion and immunity. This drink, which originates in Asia, has become a hot trend, and rightly so. Rich in antioxidants and vitamins, this healthful tea teams up with nutrient-rich blueberries, kale, and ginger to deliver a uniquely flavored smoothie.

green smoothie

high fiber

1 cup kombucha
½ cup frozen blueberries
⅓ cup avocado
2 cups baby kale (or ½ cup frozen)
2 tablespoons chia seeds
1 teaspoon ground ginger
1 to 2 pitted Medjool dates
½ to 1 cup ice

Optional Add-Ins:

Additional ½ cup frozen blueberries
1 teaspoon coconut oil
¼ teaspoon cinnamon
1 serving of your favorite protein powder

Combine all of the ingredients and blend until smooth. Serve right away.

Serves 1 | Per Serving: CALORIES: 441; TOTAL FAT: 15G; SUGAR: 39G; SODIUM: 82MG; CARBOHYDRATES: 79G; FIBER: 15G; PROTEIN: 10G

You can buy bottled kombucha, both pasteurized and unpasteurized, in various flavors in most supermarkets. You could also substitute kefir, brewed green or red tea, or Greek yogurt.

↘ Cranberries are in season in North America from October through December. Buy them when they are in season and freeze unwashed for use later in the year.

Cranberry Orange Elixir

Cranberries are known for their powerful, disease-fighting antioxidant properties, and eating them on a regular basis may boost the immune system and protect against certain types of cancer. In a creamy probiotic base of soy yogurt, this tart and sweet smoothie is bursting with nutrition.

1 cup soy yogurt
½ cup frozen cranberries
½ cup watermelon
1 small orange, peeled
¼ cup avocado
2 tablespoons hemp seeds
1 pitted Medjool date
½ to 1 cup ice

Optional Add-Ins:

1 teaspoon grated fresh ginger
1 tablespoon ground flaxseed
½ frozen banana, sliced
1 serving of your favorite protein powder

Combine all of the ingredients and blend until smooth. Serve right away.

Serves 1 | Per Serving: CALORIES: 511; TOTAL FAT: 20G; SUGAR: 47G; SODIUM: 28MG; CARBOHYDRATES: 70G; FIBER: 11G; PROTEIN: 18G

Chipper Cherry Ginger

What's not to love about cherries? Bursting with nutrition, cherries have nutrients that may work synergistically to fight cancer, stave-off gout, and decrease your risk for diabetes. Loaded in antioxidants, vitamins A, C, D, B$_6$, E, zinc, and healthy fats, this creamy smoothie is another tool in your body's defense arsenal.

½ cup Greek or soy yogurt
½ cup coconut water
1 cup frozen cherries
½ frozen banana
¼ cup almonds
2 tablespoons chia seeds
1 teaspoon grated ginger
1 pitted Medjool date
½ to 1 cup ice

Optional Add-Ins:

½ cup pineapple
2 tablespoons hemp seeds
¼ teaspoon probiotic powder
1 to 2 cups dark leafy greens

Combine all of the ingredients and blend until smooth. Serve right away.

Serves 1 | Per Serving: CALORIES: 504; TOTAL FAT: 21G; SUGAR: 51G; SODIUM: 93MG; CARBOHYDRATES: 73G; FIBER: 15G; PROTEIN: 16G

high protein

high fiber

You can substitute the yogurt and coconut water with dairy milk or a nut- or plant-based milk. If you go with plant, add back in some protein for added staying power.

You can substitute the kefir with plain Greek, soy, or coconut yogurt to retain the immune system-strengthening power of probiotics.

Lemon Blueberry Cold Buster

If a cold is getting you down, fill your blender with this immune-boosting blend. Blueberries and lemon provide vitamin C and antioxidants, and wheat germ and pumpkin seeds provide zinc. Whether you feel a cold coming on or are trying to recover faster, this smoothie is for you.

½ cup coconut water
½ cup plain kefir
1 pear, cored and sliced
1 cup frozen blueberries
2 cups baby spinach
1 tablespoon lemon juice
2 tablespoons wheat germ
1 tablespoon pumpkin seeds
1 teaspoon honey
½ to 1 cup ice

Optional Add-Ins:

½ cup frozen strawberries
1 teaspoon flax oil
½ frozen banana

Combine all of the ingredients and blend until smooth. Serve right away.

Serves 1 | Per Serving: CALORIES: 380; TOTAL FAT: 8G; SUGAR: 44G; SODIUM: 198MG; CARBOHYDRATES: 65G; FIBER: 13G; PROTEIN: 17G

Tomato Cell Support

When it comes to protecting yourself against cancer, tomatoes should be top of your list of foods to include. Tomatoes are a source of the powerful antioxidant lycopene, which can protect your DNA from damage. Not your typical smoothie ingredient, tomatoes work well with sweet berries and creamy mango.

½ cup unsweetened vanilla almond milk
½ cup plain Greek yogurt
½ cup cherry tomatoes
2 cups kale
½ cup frozen mixed berries
½ cup frozen mango
2 tablespoons chia seeds
1 teaspoon flax oil
stevia (optional)
½ to 1 cup ice

Optional Add-Ins:

½ frozen banana
1 serving protein powder
¼ cup chopped avocado

Combine all of the ingredients and blend until smooth. Serve right away.

Serves 1 | Per Serving: CALORIES: 437; TOTAL FAT: 16G; SUGAR: 27G; SODIUM:217MG; CARBOHYDRATES: 54G; FIBER: 12G; PROTEIN: 30G

veggie lover

high protein

Little tomatoes work best in smoothies, so try grape, cherry, or small Campari. Adding several small tomatoes to a smoothie won't change the flavor and will add powerful phytochemicals.

veggie lover

high protein

high fiber

↘ Hemp protein adds a concentrated source of immune-boosting omega-3 fats as well as protein and dietary fiber. Substitute with your favorite powder or replace with Greek yogurt, tofu, or soy yogurt.

Jicama Hemp Immune Support

Often referred to as the Mexican potato, jicama's mild nutty texture lends itself to just about any smoothie recipe. High in fiber and vitamin C, this smoothie is also a great source of plant-based omega-3 fats, and fruits and vegetables with anticancer properties.

1 cup unsweetened vanilla almond milk
1 serving hemp protein powder
1 cup jicama, peeled and cubed
1 apple, cored and sliced
2 cups baby spinach
½ cup avocado, chopped
1 small lime, peeled
1 pitted Medjool date
½ to 1 cup ice

Optional Add-Ins:
½ cup grated carrots
1 tablespoon hemp seeds
1 tablespoon ground flaxseed
½ cup yogurt

Combine all of the ingredients and blend until smooth. Serve right away.

Serves 1 | Per Serving: CALORIES: 495; TOTAL FAT: 21G; SUGAR: 40G; SODIUM: 247MG; CARBOHYDRATES: 74G; FIBER: 23G; PROTEIN: 14G

Lean, Mean, and Dandelion Green

If making green smoothies is going to be a regular part of your routine, consider adding the superfood spirulina to your list of pantry staples. A complete protein, this single-celled organism is loaded with essential vitamins and minerals that support health.

1 cup water
juice of ½ lemon
1 medium frozen banana, sliced
1 cup dandelion greens, stems removed
1 teaspoon spirulina
1 pitted Medjool date
½ to 1 cup ice

Optional Add-Ins:

½ cup frozen pineapple
¼ cup cilantro
1 tablespoon ground flaxseed
2 tablespoons avocado

Combine all of the ingredients and blend until smooth. Serve right away.

Serves 1 | Per Serving: CALORIES: 178; TOTAL FAT: 1G; SUGAR: 23G; SODIUM: 68MG; CARBOHYDRATES: 42G; FIBER: 6G; PROTEIN: 5G

green smoothie

low calorie

superfood star

↘ If you are new to using dandelion greens in smoothies, consider including frozen pineapple or mango for added sweetness or replace with baby spinach.

Anti-Aging and Beauty

Maintaining healthy skin while aging is something that most people want. Lifestyle factors such as not smoking, engaging in regular exercise, and using sunscreen are all important for stalling some of the visible signs of aging. But what you eat and drink matters too; in fact, it matters a lot. Filling your plate (or your blender, as the case may be) with a colorful array of fruits and vegetables will give your body an arsenal of antioxidants to fight cellular damage. Flavonoids, antioxidants, and vitamins A and C are all important for maintaining healthy skin. Eating foods such as grapes, carrots, leafy greens, green tea, citrus, low-fat dairy products, and berries can keep your skin looking younger. Zinc and selenium, minerals found in high amounts in nuts, seeds, and whole grains, can improve skin's circulation. And no anti-aging regimen would be complete without adequate sources of healthy fats such as those found in avocados, flax, hemp, and chia. Load up your blender with the following goodies and watch your skin glow!

Gorgeous Green Grape

This smoothie combines the sweet-tart flavor and unique texture of grapes with creamy and hydrating pear and a twist of citrus. Rich in resveratrol, grapes give this smoothie anti-aging clout by fighting free radicals that cause wrinkles. It also acts as a natural sunscreen.

½ cup water
½ cup silken tofu
½ frozen banana, sliced
2 cups baby kale
1 cup green seedless grapes
1 pear, cored and chopped
1 orange, peeled and quartered
2 tablespoons chia seeds
stevia (optional)
½ to 1 cup ice

Optional Add-Ins:

1 tablespoon hemp seeds
1 to 2 pitted dates
pinch nutmeg

Combine all of the ingredients and blend until smooth.
Serve right away.

Serves 1 | Per Serving: CALORIES: 457; TOTAL FAT: 8G; SUGAR: 54G; SODIUM: 92MG; CARBOHYDRATES: 94G; FIBER: 18G; PROTEIN: 16G

green smoothie

high protein

high fiber

Tofu adds a creamy texture and protein, but you can replace it with protein powder, nondairy milk or nondairy yogurt. Dairy may curdle with the citrus.

protein

↘ Grapeseed
oil contains potent
antioxidants and vitamin
E that help reduce skin
damage from the sun.
Replace with 1 teaspoon
flax oil for many of the
same benefits.

Ageless Avocado

Avocados are one of the best anti-aging foods to eat as they
are loaded in critical fatty acids, antioxidant phytonutrients,
and essential amino acids, plus they make a smoothie creamy
and delicious! With a base of skin-nourishing yogurt and
pomegranate juice, this smoothie will feed your skin from
the inside.

¼ cup 100% pomegranate juice
½ cup plain Greek yogurt
½ cup frozen peaches
½ cup frozen strawberries
½ cup chopped avocado
1 teaspoon grapeseed oil
1 teaspoon vanilla extract
½ to 1 cup ice

Optional Add-Ins:

1 tablespoon coconut flour
pinch cinnamon
1 tablespoon chia seeds

Combine all of the ingredients and blend until smooth.
Serve right away.

Serves 1 | Per Serving: CALORIES: 447; TOTAL FAT: 23G; SUGAR: 29G;
SODIUM: 72MG; CARBOHYDRATES: 39G; FIBER: 8G; PROTEIN: 22G

Glowing with Grapefruit

In addition to its delicious tangy taste, grapefruit is high in vitamin C, essential for producing collagen, which keeps your complexion plump, reducing the appearance of wrinkles. With a twist of lime, this mix is a refreshing anti-aging tonic rich in skin-protecting phytochemicals and essential fats.

½ cup 100% orange juice
½ cup silken tofu
1 pink grapefruit, peeled
½ cup frozen pineapple
1 small cucumber, sliced
½ cup chopped fresh cilantro
½ lime, peeled
1 teaspoon vanilla extract
pinch cinnamon
2 tablespoons hemp seeds
½ to 1 cup ice

Optional Add-Ins:

1 to 2 cups dark leafy greens
1 tablespoon dried goji berries
¼ cup pomegranate seeds

Combine all of the ingredients and blend until smooth. Serve right away.

Serves 1 | Per Serving: CALORIES: 377; TOTAL FAT: 10G; SUGAR: 39G; SODIUM: 43MG; CARBOHYDRATES: 61G; FIBER: 9G; PROTEIN: 15G

Many spices have skin-protective antioxidants including turmeric, cinnamon, fennel, cloves, nutmeg, ginger, coriander, and pepper. Experiment with a pinch of your favorite to find what appeals to you.

green
smoothie

high
protein

➘ Dandelion greens
are bitter, so blend them
with sweet flavorful fruits
like bananas, strawberries,
mango, citrus, and
pineapple. You can find
dandelion greens in health
food stores or forage for
them in your backyard.

Timeless Tea Toner

Apples are another skin essential as they contain copper,
which helps you make melanin, the pigment that colors your
skin and protects it from the sun's UV rays. Used with the peel
on for extra nutrients, apple is combined with creamy, protein-
filled edamame, nuts, and antioxidant-rich green tea for a
smoothie that will defy Father Time.

1 cup brewed and chilled green tea
½ frozen banana, sliced
1 green apple, cored, peel on
1 cup dandelion greens
½ cup shelled edamame
2 tablespoons walnuts
1 to 2 pitted Medjool dates
½ to 1 cup ice

Optional Add-Ins:

1 teaspoon grated ginger
½ cup Greek yogurt or silken tofu
½ cup frozen berries

Combine all of the ingredients and blend until smooth.
Serve right away.

Serves 1 | Per Serving: CALORIES: 490; TOTAL FAT: 14G; SUGAR: 60G;
SODIUM: 52MG; CARBOHYDRATES: 88G; FIBER: 14G; PROTEIN: 15G

Nectarine Naturally Glowing

Boosting your dietary intake of the mineral selenium can help protect against skin cancer, sun damage, and age spots. Just four Brazil nuts provide the recommended daily amount, making this hydrating, phytochemical-rich smoothie a perfect way to feed your skin.

1 cup coconut water
1 cup seedless red grapes
1 nectarine, pit removed
2 cups baby spinach
¼ cup Brazil nuts
1 tablespoon coconut flour
1 teaspoon vanilla extract
pinch turmeric
½ to 1 cup ice

Optional Add-Ins:

¼ teaspoon ground ginger
½ cup Greek yogurt
½ frozen banana

Combine all of the ingredients and blend until smooth. Serve right away.

Serves 1 | Per Serving: CALORIES: 475; TOTAL FAT: 22G; SUGAR: 46G; SODIUM: 224MG; CARBOHYDRATES: 53G; FIBER: 11G; PROTEIN: 11G

Coconut flour is a great thickener for smoothies and adds fiber, protein, and healthy fats. You can find coconut flour at most grocery stores in the bakery or gluten-free section.

For a creamier smoothie and an added boost of skin essential minerals zinc and selenium, add ¼ cup rolled oats. Soak them in the yogurt for a few hours in the fridge for even more texture.

Cucumber Honeydew

Applying cucumbers to your eyes is a great way to fade dark circles, but they can also feed your skin from the inside. High in free radical–fighting antioxidants and collagen-boosting vitamin C, cucumber teams up with sweet, juicy honeydew to create a high-protein shake with a hint of mint.

¾ cup Greek yogurt
1 cup cucumber, unpeeled, chopped
1 cup honeydew
1 tablespoon fresh mint, chopped
juice of ½ lime
1 tablespoon coconut flour
1 tablespoon ground flaxseed
1 pitted Medjool date
½ to 1 cup ice

Optional Add-Ins:

1 stalk celery
¼ cup chopped fresh parsley
1 tablespoon hemp seeds

Combine all of the ingredients and blend until smooth. Serve right away.

Serves 1 | Per Serving: CALORIES: 334; TOTAL FAT: 7G; SUGAR: 37G; SODIUM: 105MG; CARBOHYDRATES: 50G; FIBER: 9G; PROTEIN: 20G

Beta Carotene Age Buster

meal swap

Energy boosting and delicious, you might be surprised how quickly your skin responds to the influx of nutrients from this age-busting smoothie. High in carotenoids, vitamins A and C, and essential fats, you and your skin will love this thick and delicious smoothie with a tropical flare.

½ cup water
½ cup soy yogurt
½ cup papaya
½ cup frozen mango
1 medium carrot, chopped
1 pear, cored, peel on
1 orange, peeled
1 teaspoon coconut oil
1 teaspoon grated ginger
½ to 1 cup ice

Optional Add-Ins:

1 tablespoon coconut flour
¼ cup pomegranate seeds
1 to 2 cups dark leafy greens
pinch mace

 If you don't have a high-powered blender, use grated carrots or substitute the water with 100% carrot juice.

Combine all of the ingredients and blend until smooth.
Serve right away.

Serves 1 | Per Serving: CALORIES: 410; TOTAL FAT: 8G; SUGAR: 59G; SODIUM: 60MG; CARBOHYDRATES: 83G; FIBER: 14G; PROTEIN: 9G

For a different
variation with a dose
of phytochemicals,
replace the ginger with
unsweetened cacao and
add cherries. Cherries,
beets, and cacao make an
awesome trio of flavors.

Beauty with Berries and Beets

A skin regimen wouldn't be complete without the nutritional
punch of berries and beets. High in vitamins, minerals, and
cell-protecting phytochemicals, this smoothie gets added skin
protection from zinc, and *pepitas,* filled with vitamin E. Sip
your way to a clear complexion with this very berry, creamy,
and delicious shake.

½ cup unsweetened almond milk
½ cup Greek yogurt
⅓ cup frozen blueberries
⅓ cup frozen raspberries
⅓ cup frozen strawberries
¼ cup beet, steamed and peeled
¼ cup avocado, chopped
2 tablespoons pumpkin seeds (*pepitas*)
1 teaspoon grated fresh ginger
stevia (optional)
½ to 1 cup ice

Optional Add-Ins:
1 tablespoon goji berries
½ cup frozen cherries
1 to 2 cups leafy greens
½ frozen banana

Combine all of the ingredients and blend until smooth.
Serve right away.

Serves 1 | Per Serving: CALORIES: 418; TOTAL FAT: 19G; SUGAR: 34G;
SODIUM: 162MG; CARBOHYDRATES: 50G; FIBER: 11G; PROTEIN: 17G

Apple Cherry Pumpkin Tea

Full of wrinkle-reducing free radical–fighting superfoods, this creamy and colorful smoothie uses African red tea, also known as rooibos, to kick the nutritional power up a notch. Skin-nourishing coconut flour, pumpkin, and almonds are used to add a creamy texture, and cherries add a sweet and delicious taste.

1 cup brewed and chilled rooibos tea
1 cup frozen cherries
1 red apple, cored, peel on
¼ cup canned pumpkin (not pie mix)
¼ cup almonds
1 tablespoon coconut flour
1 serving pea protein (or your favorite protein)
¼ teaspoon cinnamon
1 pitted Medjool date
½ to 1 cup ice

Optional Add-Ins:

1 teaspoon açai powder
1 teaspoon flax oil
¼ cup rolled oats
1 tablespoon goji berries

Combine all of the ingredients and blend until smooth. Serve right away.

Serves 1 | Per Serving: CALORIES: 534; TOTAL FAT: 2G; SUGAR: 53G; SODIUM: 72MG; CARBOHYDRATES: 78G; FIBER: 17G; PROTEIN: 33G

You can use any type of tea as all teas have a unique array of beneficial phytochemicals and antioxidants. You could also use ½ cup 100% tart cherry juice for a concentrated source of nutrients.

↘ For even more
anti-aging benefits,
experiment with different
herbs and spices, including
cinnamon, turmeric,
ginger, cloves, and basil.

Blueberry Mango Bean

If you want healthy locks, glowing skin, and strong nails,
markers of overall health, the best thing you can do is to follow
a healthy diet. This refreshing high-protein smoothie is high in
B vitamins, particularly biotin, which plays a major role in hair
health. Skip the supplements and nourish yourself with whole
foods instead.

¾ cup water
½ cup Greek yogurt
1 cup baby spinach
½ cup frozen blueberries
½ cup frozen mango
½ frozen banana
¼ cup kidney beans
2 tablespoons almonds
1 teaspoon ground flaxseed
stevia (optional)
½ to 1 cup water

Optional Add-Ins:
1 teaspoon açai powder
¼ cup chopped avocado
1 tablespoon wheat germ
1 tablespoon wheat bran

Combine all of the ingredients and blend until smooth.
Serve right away.

Serves 1 | Per Serving: CALORIES: 459; TOTAL FAT: 10G; SUGAR: 31G;
SODIUM: 64MG; CARBOHYDRATES: 73G; FIBER: 14G; PROTEIN: 26G

Anti-Aging Pineapple Green Smoothie

meal swap

This luscious anti-aging green smoothie blends enzyme-rich pineapple with potassium-rich banana, creamy fiber-rich avocado, vitamin- and mineral-rich leafy greens, and spicy ginger to deliver a delicious way to protect your body against premature aging and chronic inflammation. With added selenium from Brazil nuts, enjoy this healing drink on a weekly basis.

1 cup unsweetened vanilla almond milk
1 cup frozen pineapple chunks
½ frozen banana, sliced
¼ cup chopped avocado
1 cup romaine lettuce
¼ teaspoon turmeric
½ teaspoon grated fresh ginger
½ tablespoon lime juice
2 tablespoons Brazil nuts
1 pitted Medjool date
½ to 1 cup water

Optional Add-Ins:

1 tablespoon ground flaxseed
½ cup silken tofu
1 teaspoon honey

Combine all of the ingredients and blend until smooth. Serve right away.

You can substitute the romaine with any nutritious fresh green, including spinach, kale, dandelion greens, endive, arugula, or Swiss chard.

Serves 1 | Per Serving: CALORIES: 554; TOTAL FAT: 21G; SUGAR: 77G; SODIUM: 192MG; CARBOHYDRATES: 96G; FIBER: 11G; PROTEIN: 6G

Muscle, Bone, and Joint Support

Staying active throughout your life means keeping your muscles, bones, and joints in good shape. From the time you are born until about age 30, your muscles grow larger and stronger. But if your physical activity routine goes by the wayside in your 30s, you can lose as much as five percent of your muscle mass per decade! And since muscles support your joints, if you don't have enough muscle…well, you get the idea. As with all things health-related, prevention is key, and two smart strategies are to have a regular program of cardiovascular and strength training, and to follow a varied and balanced diet. Some key nutrients to support your musculature include protein, calcium, vitamins D and K, essential fats, antioxidants, and phytochemicals. If you already have joint pain or a condition like gout or rheumatoid arthritis, including spices such as turmeric and ginger can help ease pain and inflammation.

Spicy Arthritis Ammunition

This creamy, golden, orangey smoothie is full of phytochemicals and antioxidants to give your joints a dose of TLC. In a refreshing calcium- and vitamin D–rich base, this delicious smoothie combines the sweet taste and healing powers of pineapple with inflammation-reducing spices.

½ cup unsweetened almond milk
½ cup Greek yogurt (or soy yogurt)
⅔ cup frozen banana, sliced (about 1 medium)
1 cup frozen pineapple
1 large carrot, chopped (about 1 cup)
1¼ teaspoon ground tumeric
1 tablespoon grated fresh ginger
½ teaspoon ground cinnamon
1 teaspoon vanilla extract
2 tablespoons hemp seeds
½ to 1 cup ice

Optional Add-Ins:

1 tablespoon chia seed gel
1 to 2 cups dark leafy greens
1 tablespoon ground flaxseed

Combine all of the ingredients and blend until smooth. Serve right away.

Serves 1 | Per Serving: CALORIES: 438; TOTAL FAT: 11G; SUGAR: 45G; SODIUM: 175MG; CARBOHYDRATES: 68G; FIBER: 11G; PROTEIN: 18G

meal swap

high protein

superfood star

Its best to start slow with turmeric to avoid upsetting your stomach. Gradually increase the amount you use over time to boost the anti-inflammatory power of this smoothie.

Blueberries contain compounds that can reduce muscle soreness and can be substituted for the more expensive cherries. You can also use any nut butter or replace nut butter with 2 tablespoons whole nuts.

Sunflower Chocolate Muscle Builder

An ideal post-workout drink should include high-quality protein, but not too much, as well as complex carbohydrates, healthy fats, antioxidants, phytochemicals, and simple sugars to aid in the absorption of the nutrients into muscle. This scrumptious muscle-recovery smoothie has all that and more!

¾ cup protein-fortified almond, soy, or dairy milk
½ cup Greek yogurt
1 cup frozen cherries
¼ cup rolled oats
1 tablespoon unsweetened cacao or cocoa
1 tablespoon unsweetened sunflower seed butter
1 tablespoon ground flaxseed
1 to 2 pitted Medjool dates
½ to 1 cup ice

Optional Add-Ins:

¼ cup avocado
½ frozen banana
1 tablespoon hemp seed
¼ teaspoon cinnamon

Combine all of the ingredients and blend until smooth. Serve right away.

Serves 1 | Per Serving: CALORIES: 543; TOTAL FAT: 17G; SUGAR: 56G; SODIUM: 159MG; CARBOHYDRATES: 86G; FIBER: 12G; PROTEIN: 21G

Apricot Avenger

The unassuming apricot is rich in potent plant antioxidants with protective effects while being very low in calories. Apricots, which are high in fiber, rival green tea for their catechin content and contain powerful anti-inflammatory phytochemicals. Paired with omega-3 fats and plant-based protein, this smoothie will keep you on the right track towards health.

high protein

1 cup coconut water
4 medium apricots, pitted and chopped
½ cup frozen peaches
¼ cup avocado
1 tablespoon chia seeds
1 teaspoon vanilla extract
1 serving pea protein (or your favorite protein)
½ to 1 cup ice

Optional Add-Ins:
1 to 2 cups dark leafy greens
½ frozen banana
½ cup yogurt

Combine all of the ingredients and blend until smooth.
Serve right away.

Look for apricots and peaches with a rich orange color while avoiding those that are pale and yellow. Fruits should be slightly soft, as a fully ripened fruit has the most antioxidants.

Serves 1 | Per Serving: CALORIES: 370; TOTAL FAT: 13G; SUGAR: 30G; SODIUM: 220MG; CARBOHYDRATES: 34G; FIBER: 9G; PROTEIN: 27G

meal
swap

high
protein

high
fiber

To keep the high-quality protein content and make this vegan, use soy milk and replace the yogurt and cottage cheese with silken tofu.

Almond Joint Joy

With a mix of slow-digesting muscle-feeding proteins, this smoothie contains essential nutrients needed to support muscle, joint, and bone health, and it tastes almost too good to be healthy. High in calcium, vitamins D and E, magnesium, potassium, and healthy fats, enjoy this as a breakfast, post-workout meal, or hearty snack.

¾ cup unsweetened almond milk
½ cup cottage cheese
½ cup yogurt
1 frozen banana, sliced
2 tablespoons unsweetened cacao or cocoa
2 tablespoons almond butter
2 tablespoons unsweetened shredded coconut
1 tablespoon chia seeds
1 pitted Medjool date
½ to 1 cup ice

Optional Add-Ins:
Cacao nibs, for garnish
Sliced almonds, for garnish
½ cup frozen berries

Combine all of the ingredients and blend until smooth. Serve right away.

Serves 1 | Per Serving: CALORIES: 737; TOTAL FAT: 37G; SUGAR: 41G; SODIUM: 688MG; CARBOHYDRATES: 77G; FIBER: 15G; PROTEIN: 36G

Mango Muscle

High in cell-repairing carotenoids from mango, this smoothie gets added nutrition from wheat germ. Wheat germ contains folic acid and vitamin E for cell growth and development, and green veggies provide bone- and joint-supporting vitamins A, C, and K. In a tasty base rich in electrolytes, this smoothie is better than a multivitamin.

¾ cup coconut water
½ cup Greek yogurt
1 cup frozen mango
½ cup frozen banana
2 cups baby spinach (or ½ cup frozen)
½ cup raw zucchini
2 tablespoons wheat germ
½ to 1 cup ice

Optional Add-Ins:

¼ cup rolled oats
1 tablespoon hemp seed
½ cup frozen berries

Combine all of the ingredients and blend until smooth. Serve right away.

Serves 1 | Per Serving: CALORIES: 338; TOTAL FAT: 4G; SUGAR: 45G; SODIUM: 207MG; CARBOHYDRATES: 58G; FIBER: 9G; PROTEIN: 19G

high protein

↘ For lower sugar and more bone-supporting calcium, protein, and vitamin D, replace the coconut water with dairy, soy, or protein-fortified almond milk.

Maca is rich
in B vitamins and
phytochemicals and may
help boost energy levels
and play a role in immune
function. While not a direct
substitute, replace it with
2 tablespoons ground
flaxseed.

Post-Workout Maca Ginger

Easy to make and digest, smoothies offer a simple way to get the protein and carbs you need to build muscle, and the antioxidants to fight inflammation and damage. You'll get a hit of powerful phytochemicals from the spices used in this smoothie, while the protein and healthy fats from the tofu and seeds satisfy hunger.

1 cup protein-fortified almond milk (or fat-free milk)
½ cup silken tofu
½ frozen banana
½ cup frozen blueberries
2 cups dark leafy greens
¼ cup pumpkin seeds
1 teaspoon grated fresh ginger
1 teaspoon maca root powder
½ teaspoon ground cinnamon
¼ teaspoon ground turmeric
1 teaspoon flax oil
1 to 2 pitted Medjool dates

Optional Add-Ins:
¼ teaspoon spirulina
¼ cup cooked quinoa
1 tablespoon chia seed gel

Combine all of the ingredients and blend until smooth. Serve right away.

Serves 1 | Per Serving: CALORIES: 597; TOTAL FAT: 25G; SUGAR: 55G; SODIUM: 231MG; CARBOHYDRATES: 86G; FIBER: 11G; PROTEIN: 18G

Parsley Power

The ultimate green smoothie for reducing inflammation and easing joint and muscle pain, the trifecta of creaminess—yogurt, avocado, and pear—serve as the base for powerful anti-inflammatory spices and green veggies. A perfect nutrient-dense drink to target your health needs.

½ cup water
½ cup Greek yogurt
⅓ cup avocado, chopped
½ cup frozen pineapple
1 medium pear, cored and chopped
1 stalk celery
½ cup chopped fresh parsley
1 medium carrot, chopped
¼ teaspoon ground turmeric
1 teaspoon ground ginger
stevia (optional)
½ to 1 cup ice

Optional Add-Ins:

1 teaspoon coconut oil
2 tablespoons ground flaxseed
1 to 2 cups dark leafy greens

Combine all of the ingredients and blend until smooth. Serve right away.

Serves 1 | Per Serving: CALORIES: 355; TOTAL FAT: 12G; SUGAR: 33G; SODIUM: 110MG; CARBOHYDRATES: 53G; FIBER: 13G; PROTEIN: 13G

veggie lover

green smoothie

superfood star

high protein

High in vitamins A and K and anti-inflammatory compounds, the taste of celery can easily overpower a smoothie. Start with one stalk and combine with a sweet fruit.

veggie
lover

meal
swap

high
protein

↘ For a creamier smoothie higher in fiber, healthy fats, and complex carbohydrates for muscle repair, add ¼ cup rolled oats and 2 tablespoons chopped avocado.

Beet Cranberry Crusher

Power up your workouts with this electrolyte- and phytochemical-rich, creamy smoothie. Beets are high in nitrates, which studies show improve blood flow and boost endurance. Loaded in plant-based proteins and healthy fats, add this smoothie to your muscle health arsenal.

1 cup silken tofu
½ cup coconut water
½ cup frozen cranberries
1 small beet, raw or roasted, chopped (about ¼ cup)
½ frozen banana
½ medium cucumber
1 celery stalk
1 cup baby kale
1 to 2 pitted Medjool dates
½ to 1 cup ice

Optional Add-Ins:
¼ cup chopped avocado
2 tablespoons chia seeds
1 teaspoon grated ginger
1 orange

Combine all of the ingredients and blend until smooth. Serve right away.

Serves 1 | Per Serving: CALORIES: 359; TOTAL FAT: 3G; SUGAR: 53G; SODIUM: 195MG; CARBOHYDRATES: 75G; FIBER: 10G; PROTEIN: 11G

Orange Broccoli Bone Builder

Oranges are one of the most calcium-rich fruits available, and we all know calcium is important for healthy bones. But did you know that magnesium and vitamins D and K are too? Dates, hemp, and bananas fit the bill for magnesium, leafy greens and broccoli provide vitamin K, and almond milk provides vitamin D, all served up in a creamy shake.

1 cup unsweetened almond milk
1 medium orange, peeled and chopped
½ frozen banana
1 serving hemp protein powder (or your favorite)
½ cup frozen broccoli
2 cups dark leafy greens
2 tablespoons hemp seeds
½ teaspoon vanilla extract
1 to 2 pitted Medjool dates
½ to 1 cup ice

Optional Add-Ins:

½ cup frozen berries
½ cup yogurt
1 medium carrot

Combine all of the ingredients and blend until smooth.
Serve right away.

Serves 1 | Per Serving: CALORIES: 497; TOTAL FAT: 14G; SUGAR: 58G; SODIUM: 251MG; CARBOHYDRATES: 82G; FIBER: 15G; PROTEIN: 20G

meal swap

high protein

high fiber

 Protein is needed to support healthy muscles and bones, but you don't need to use powder. Replace with dairy or soy yogurt, beans, or tofu.

Pumpkin Cherry Joint Juice

If you have gout, a painful form of arthritis, following a diet low in purines can prevent blood levels of uric acid from getting too high. You won't feel deprived with this low-purine smoothie made with a gout-reducing superstar, cherries, combined with a mix of anti-inflammatory foods.

½ cup 100% tart cherry juice
½ cup low-fat Greek yogurt
½ cup frozen strawberries
½ cup frozen cherries
¼ cup canned pumpkin puree (not pie mix)
1 teaspoon flax oil
2 tablespoons walnuts
1 teaspoon grated fresh ginger
½ to 1 cup ice

Optional Add-Ins:
¼ cup rolled oats
½ cup silken tofu
¼ cup beans
1 to 2 cups baby spinach

Combine all of the ingredients and blend until smooth. Serve right away.

Serves 1 | Per Serving: CALORIES: 409; TOTAL FAT: 16G; SUGAR: 51G; SODIUM: 80MG; CARBOHYDRATES: 61G; FIBER: 6G; PROTEIN: 10G

Both cherries and low-fat dairy products have been shown to reduce uric acid levels in the blood. For extra nutrition, add an additional ½ cup skim milk or more yogurt.

Cashew Cream

When it comes to supporting bone and joint health, cashews are a standout with their high copper and magnesium content, two minerals essential to bone and joint flexibility and muscle tone regulation. With the added benefit of high-quality protein and essential fats, this smoothie makes a great breakfast or post-workout shake.

1 cup unsweetened vanilla almond milk
½ cup cottage cheese
½ cup frozen raspberries
1 cup spinach
2 tablespoons ground flaxseed
2 tablespoons cashews
¼ cup rolled oats
¼ teaspoon ground cinnamon
1 pitted Medjool date
½ to 1 cup ice

For garnish:
1 pitted and sliced Medjool date

Optional Add-Ins:
1 serving protein powder
¼ cup beans
1 tablespoon cashew butter

Combine all of the ingredients and blend until smooth.
Serve right away.

Serves 1 | Per Serving: CALORIES: 595; TOTAL FAT: 19G; SUGAR: 46G; SODIUM: 672MG; CARBOHYDRATES: 82G; FIBER: 16G; PROTEIN: 27G

meal swap

high protein

high fiber

You can use Greek yogurt in place of the cottage cheese but increase the quantity to 1 cup to keep the same amount of protein.

↘ To make this a complete meal replacement, add a serving of protein in the form of powder, yogurt, tofu, beans, or cottage cheese.

Blueberry Ginger Joint Ease

With the power of muscle soreness–reducing blueberries and anti-inflammatory ginger, this smoothie is high in free radical–fighting antioxidants and phytochemicals. With added omega-3 fats and vitamin E from almonds and hemp, the ingredients work synergistically to quiet inflammation, reduce pain, and speed recovery from tough workouts.

1 cup unsweetened protein-fortified vanilla almond milk
1 cup kale
1 cup spinach
½ frozen banana
½ cup frozen blueberries
1 tablespoon almond butter
1 tablespoon hemp seeds
1 teaspoon freshly grated ginger
1 pitted Medjool date
½ to 1 cup ice

Optional Add-Ins:
½ cup silken tofu
½ cup Greek yogurt
1 teaspoon flax oil

Combine all of the ingredients and blend until smooth. Serve right away.

Serves 1 | Per Serving: CALORIES: 390; TOTAL FAT: 16G; SUGAR: 32G; SODIUM: 234MG; CARBOHYDRATES: 57G; FIBER: 9G; PROTEIN: 12G

Crunchy Nutty Goji Berry

Considered both a fruit and an herb, goji berries add antioxidant power to this calcium– and vitamin D–rich smoothie. With pain-reducing quercitin from cherries, and bone-building vitamin K from celery, this creamy high-protein smoothie will help ward off muscle soreness and fatigue.

1 cup unsweetened almond milk
½ cup Greek yogurt
1 cup celery, chopped
½ cup frozen cherries
½ cup goji berries
2 tablespoons chia seeds
2 tablespoons natural crunchy peanut butter
¼ cup cooked quinoa
1 pitted Medjool date
½ to 1 cup ice

Optional Add-Ins:

¼ cup chopped avocado
½ frozen banana
pinch ground cinnamon
1 to 2 cups baby spinach

Combine all of the ingredients and blend until smooth. Serve right away.

Serves 1 | Per Serving: CALORIES: 639; TOTAL FAT: 30G; SUGAR: 46G; SODIUM: 360MG; CARBOHYDRATES: 80G; FIBER: 16G; PROTEIN: 27G

meal swap

high protein

high fiber

The quinoa adds high-quality carbs, but you can substitute with rolled oats, or simply increase the amount of frozen fruit you use.

Heart Healthy

When it comes to eating well to keep your cholesterol in check and your heart and arteries in good shape, you probably know to cut down on your saturated fat and salt intake, increase your fiber intake, eat more fruits and vegetables, and enjoy fatty fish a couple of times a week. If you translate that to mean "tasteless, boring food," think again. Smoothies, when prepared with the right ingredients and the right amounts, can provide a daily dose of fiber, omega-3 fatty acids, phytochemicals, vitamins, minerals, and antioxidants. Smoothies don't taste like burgers and fries, but you might be surprised how delicious they can be and how good they can make you feel. Some of the top heart-healthy ingredients featured in the following recipes include apples, bananas, cacao, oats, dairy products, soy, winter squash, wheat germ, flaxseed, and avocado, with a dash of flavor from cinnamon, ginger, turmeric, and clove. Enjoy!

Clementine Cholesterol Crusher

This sweet and creamy smoothie is a great addition to a heart-healthy eating plan. High in cholesterol-lowering soluble fiber and pectin, vitamin C, potassium, and healthy fats, drinking this smoothie is a great way to jump-start your heart and your day.

1 cup plain soy milk
3 clementines, peeled
1 apple, peeled, cored, and chopped
2 cups spinach
2 tablespoons wheat germ
¼ cup avocado, chopped
¼ teaspoon almond extract
1 pitted Medjool date
½ to 1 cup ice

Optional Add-Ins:
¼ teaspoon turmeric
½ frozen banana
½ cup frozen berries

Combine all of the ingredients and blend until smooth. Serve right away.

Serves 1 | Per Serving: CALORIES: 525; TOTAL FAT: 14G; SUGAR: 64G; SODIUM: 177MG; CARBOHYDRATES: 93G; FIBER: 18G; PROTEIN: 17G

high protein

high fiber

 Avocados are a quintessential smoothie ingredient, so when you see a deal, stock up and freeze them. Simply wash the outside, cut, peel, chop, and store in zip-top bags for up to five months.

Soaking your nuts makes them more digestible and adds a creamier texture. Simply soak for a few hours in water or overnight, drain, discard the soaking liquid, and add to your smoothie.

Berry Heart Healthy

This berry delicious smoothie provides a hearty dose of phytochemicals, antioxidants, healthy fats, and fiber that will energize you and help you stay on track with a healthy-eating plan. With a dash of flavanol-rich cacao, keeping your heart healthy never tasted so good.

½ cup unsweetened almond milk
½ cup Greek yogurt
½ frozen banana, sliced
1 cup frozen blueberries
2 cups baby kale
¼ cup rolled oats, soaked
1 tablespoon unsweetened cacao or cocoa
2 tablespoons almonds
stevia (optional)
½ to 1 cup ice

Optional Add-Ins:

2 tablespoons ground flaxseed
½ cup cherries
2 tablespoons avocado

Combine all of the ingredients and blend until smooth. Serve right away.

Serves 1 | Per Serving: CALORIES: 455; TOTAL FAT: 12G; SUGAR: 26G; SODIUM: 185MG; CARBOHYDRATES: 73G; FIBER: 13G; PROTEIN: 23G

Sweet Potato Carrot Potassium Punch

veggie lover

high protein

Most people get too much sodium and not enough potassium, and studies show that boosting your intake of potassium can drastically reduce your risk for stroke and lower your risk for heart disease. Each yummy ingredient in this smoothie is a potassium superstar.

¼ cup 100% pomegranate juice
1 cup Greek yogurt
1 medium sweet potato, cooked (about ⅔ cup mashed)
½ frozen banana
¼ cup avocado, chopped
1 medium carrot, chopped (about ⅔ cup)
2 pitted prunes, chopped
1 teaspoon molasses
¼ teaspoon coriander
½ to 1 cup ice

Optional Add-Ins:

1 to 2 cups baby spinach
1 tablespoon ground flaxseed
1 tablespoon chia seeds
½ cup papaya

Combine all of the ingredients and blend until smooth. Serve right away.

Orange juice is high in potassium and can be substituted for the more expensive pomegranate juice. Just plan on drinking your smoothie soon after you make it as dairy and citrus sometimes separate.

Serves 1 | Per Serving: CALORIES: 502; TOTAL FAT: 12G; SUGAR: 44G; SODIUM: 156MG; CARBOHYDRATES: 79G; FIBER: 11G; PROTEIN: 25G

Walnut Wellness

Eating nuts is good for your heart and can reduce your bad (LDL) cholesterol, improve the health of your artery linings, and reduce your risk of blood clots. Plus, nuts are tasty and they add a rich and delicious flavor to smoothies. Full of fiber, vitamin E, and healthy fats, there is a lot of nutrition packed into this drink.

⬊ Cottage cheese is an excellent source of high-quality protein but it is high in sodium. If you can't find a low-sodium version, replace it with Greek yogurt or silken tofu. Rinsing works too, but will remove much of the calcium.

½ cup unsweetened almond milk
½ cup low-sodium cottage cheese
½ cup frozen raspberries
2 medium apricots, sliced
½ frozen banana
¼ cup walnuts
¼ teaspoon ground ginger
¼ teaspoon cinnamon
⅛ teaspoon cloves
1 teaspoon flax oil
1 pitted Medjool date
½ to 1 cup ice

Optional Add-Ins:

1 to 2 cups dark leafy greens
1 tablespoon wheat germ
½ apple

Combine all of the ingredients and blend until smooth. Serve right away.

Serves 1 | Per Serving: CALORIES: 637; TOTAL FAT: 27G; SUGAR: 64G; SODIUM: 324MG; CARBOHYDRATES: 84G; FIBER: 13G; PROTEIN: 26G

Chocolate Cherry Circulation Soother

high protein

Studies indicate that tart cherries may help lower cholesterol and triglycerides, reduce inflammation, and improve belly fat—all factors linked to heart disease. With a boost of antioxidants from grapes and cacao, and a dose of omega-3 fats, this smoothie is packed with heart-healthy compounds.

½ cup 100% red grape juice
½ cup Greek yogurt
1 cup frozen cherries
1 cup kale
1 tablespoon almond butter
2 tablespoons chia seeds
1 teaspoon maca
1 tablespoon cacao
¼ teaspoon cinnamon
½ to 1 cup ice

Optional Add-Ins:

2 tablespoons dried tart cherries
½ cup seedless red grapes
¼ cup chopped avocado
1 tablespoon ground flaxseed

Combine all of the ingredients and blend until smooth. Serve right away.

Maca is a root that grows in the mountains of Peru. It contains iron and can help restore red blood cells, which can help fight cardiovascular diseases. While not an equal substitution, replace with wheat germ, flaxseed, or hemp.

Serves 1 | Per Serving: CALORIES: 444; TOTAL FAT: 17G; SUGAR: 39G; SODIUM: 74MG; CARBOHYDRATES: 63G; FIBER: 11G; PROTEIN: 21G

If you can't find rice bran, which contains a mix of soluble and insoluble fiber, substitute with psyllium husk, oat bran, wheat bran, or a mix of all three.

Feel Good Flax and Fiber

Loaded in fiber and heart-healthy omega-3 fats, this smoothie has a velvety consistency and light sweet taste from the combination of peaches, beans, oats, and seeds. Peaches contain phenolic compounds that can keep cholesterol levels in check, upping the nutritional power of this meal in a glass.

1 cup soy milk
½ cup Greek yogurt
1 cup frozen peaches
¼ cup white beans
½ cup rolled oats
2 tablespoons ground flaxseed
1 tablespoon chia seeds
1 teaspoon rice bran
¼ teaspoon cinnamon
1 pitted Medjool date
½ to 1 cup ice

Optional Add-Ins:

½ cup frozen berries
½ frozen banana
¼ cup chopped avocado
1 to 2 cups dark leafy greens

Combine all of the ingredients and blend until smooth. Serve right away.

Serves 1 | Per Serving: CALORIES: 672; TOTAL FAT: 17G; SUGAR: 45G; SODIUM: 272MG; CARBOHYDRATES: 101G; FIBER: 20G; PROTEIN: 34G

Blueberry Banana Cocoa Bean

Black beans and cocoa team up in this heart-healthy smoothie powered by plant-based protein. Black beans are an excellent source of cholesterol-lowering fiber and heart-health promoting B vitamins, and they contribute an amazing creamy texture. Rich in flavanols, potassium, and omega-3 fats, you'll be amazed at how delicious this tastes.

1 cup unsweetened vanilla almond milk
½ frozen banana, sliced
½ cup frozen blueberries
½ cup black beans
1 tablespoon hemp seeds
1 tablespoon unsweetened cocoa
1 tablespoon ground flaxseed
1 teaspoon ground cinnamon
1 to 2 pitted Medjool dates
½ to 1 cup ice

Optional Add-Ins:
¼ cup chopped avocado
1 tablespoon chia seeds
1 cup dark leafy greens

Combine all of the ingredients and blend until smooth. Serve right away.

Serves 1 | Per Serving: CALORIES: 473; TOTAL FAT: 11G; SUGAR: 48G; SODIUM: 200MG; CARBOHYDRATES: 87G; FIBER: 19G; PROTEIN: 15G

superfood star

high protein

high fiber

To increase the protein content, reduce the almond milk to ½ cup and add ½ cup Greek yogurt, cottage cheese, or silken tofu.

Açai can be
purchased in flash-
pasteurized smoothie
packets in the refrigerated
section of your grocery
or health food store.
Substitute with any
other berry.

Açai Apple Avocado

Do you know why an apple a day keeps the doctor away?
Because apples are an excellent source of cholesterol-lowering
pectin and can help fight C-reactive protein, which can
increase the risk of heart disease. Rich in fiber, omega-3 fats,
vitamins E and C, potassium, and antioxidants, this filling
shake is chock-full of superfoods.

1 cup unsweetened almond milk
1 apple, cored and chopped
½ cup frozen açai berries
½ cup frozen kale (or 2 cups fresh)
¼ cup chopped avocado
2 tablespoons hemp seeds
1 tablespoon psyllium husk
1 to 2 pitted Medjool dates
½ to 1 cup ice

Optional Add-Ins:
½ cup Greek yogurt
½ frozen banana
½ cup silken tofu

Combine all of the ingredients and blend until smooth.
Serve right away.

Serves 1 | Per Serving: CALORIES: 718; TOTAL FAT: 18G; SUGAR: 51G;
SODIUM: 381MG; CARBOHYDRATES: 106G; FIBER: 41G; PROTEIN: 54G

Orange Omegas

This smoothie takes its flavor inspiration from a popular mall chain but transforms the ingredients into a shake with heart-protecting superpowers. High in potassium, vitamins C and D, calcium, omega-3 fats, and fiber, this smoothie makes a refreshing afternoon snack on a hot summer day.

1 cup soy milk
6 ounces frozen orange juice concentrate
2 medium oranges, peeled
1 small yellow squash, sliced (about 1 cup)
2 tablespoons ground flaxseed
1 teaspoon vanilla extract
1 pitted Medjool date
½ to 1 cup ice

Optional Add-Ins:
¼ cup chopped avocado
1 serving protein powder
1 tablespoon hemp seeds
½ cup frozen mango

Combine all of the ingredients and blend until smooth. Serve right away.

Serves 1 | Per Serving: CALORIES: 759; TOTAL FAT: 10G; SUGAR: 129G; SODIUM: 154MG; CARBOHYDRATES: 153G; FIBER: 19G; PROTEIN: 21G

high
protein

high
fiber

You can substitute the yellow squash with ½ cup canned pumpkin or a medium sweet potato, cooked mashed, for even more potassium, fiber, and phytochemicals.

You can use raw or toasted wheat germ in any of the recipes. Wheat germ is toasted to increase the shelf life and make it more digestible. It is also slightly lower in fat.

Raspberry Heart Smart

This creamy, sweet smoothie is exactly what the doctor ordered to keep your heart healthy. Rich in blood pressure–lowering potassium from dairy and banana, with flavanols from cocoa for a healthy circulatory system, and cholesterol-lowering almonds and wheat germ, this smoothie is delicious and definitely heart smart.

½ cup nonfat milk
½ cup nonfat Greek yogurt
½ frozen banana, sliced
½ cup frozen raspberries
1 teaspoon unsweetened cocoa
1 tablespoon almond butter
1 tablespoon wheat germ
½ teaspoon vanilla extract
stevia (optional)
½ to 1 cup ice

Optional Add-Ins:

¼ cup chopped avocado
1 tablespoon hemp seeds
1 teaspoon flax oil

Combine all of the ingredients and blend until smooth. Serve right away.

Serves 1 | Per Serving: CALORIES: 430; TOTAL FAT: 10G; SUGAR: 46G; SODIUM: 110MG; CARBOHYDRATES: 64G; FIBER: 9G; PROTEIN: 23G

Pomegranate Beet

Beets have become an athlete's best friend due to their high nitrate content and ability to improve blood flow to working muscles. Now a new study shows that beets can also improve blood flow to the heart and reduce blood pressure. In a nitrate-rich base of pomegranate juice, this smoothie may be an inexpensive way to keep blood pressure in check.

½ cup 100% pomegranate juice
½ cup water
½ cup frozen strawberries
2 cups spinach
¼ cup peeled and grated raw beet
1 apple, cored and chopped
2 tablespoons almonds
1 teaspoon grated fresh ginger
½ teaspoon fresh lime juice
½ to 1 cup ice

Optional Add-Ins:
¼ cup chopped avocado
½ frozen banana
½ cup Greek yogurt

Combine all of the ingredients and blend until smooth. Serve right away.

Serves 1 | Per Serving: CALORIES: 377; TOTAL FAT: 7G; SUGAR: 60G; SODIUM: 96MG; CARBOHYDRATES: 79G; FIBER: 10G; PROTEIN: 6G

superfood star

To boost the nitrate content further, add one or more of the following foods: arugula, spinach, celery, and lettuce. Fruits tend to be lower in nitrates but strawberries are a good source.

Smoothies for Overall Wellness

The recipes in this chapter will wake up your taste buds, present more flavor and ingredient combinations for you to enjoy, and help you make customizations to suit your personal tastes. If you have a craving for a particular muffin, pie, or cake, chances are you can create a nutritious smoothie version by using whole, unprocessed, clean ingredients. Each smoothie includes protein for the satiety factor, fruits and/or veggies, herbs, spices, and a variety of thickeners and sweeteners. Designed with overall wellness and health in mind, each recipe will give your body the energy it craves on the day of a tough workout. Hungry for a high-fat store-bought blueberry muffin? Make a healthy smoothie instead! Never had a smoothie made with calming lavender before? It it might be time to teach your blender some new tricks. Use the Mix-and-Match charts in Chapter 1, optional add-ins, and substitution tips to tweak the recipes and make them your own.

Gingerbread Goodness

Gingerbread gets its distinctive taste from blackstrap molasses, which, unlike other sugars, is high in iron, magnesium, calcium, and copper. Molasses is also considered safe for diabetics and has a moderate glycemic index. With added creaminess from fruit, nuts, and seeds, this smoothie is like eating a bowl of gingerbread.

½ cup almond milk
½ cup Greek yogurt
½ frozen banana, sliced
1 pear, cored and sliced
1 tablespoon almond butter
1 tablespoon chia gel
1 tablespoon molasses
1 teaspoon grated fresh ginger
¼ teaspoon ground cinnamon
⅛ teaspoon nutmeg
⅛ teaspoon cardamom
½ to 1 cup ice

Molasses has a very strong distinctive flavor, so you may want to start with ½ tablespoon. Then, taste your smoothie and decide how much more you want to add.

Optional Add-Ins:
2 tablespoons crushed graham cracker crumbs
1 serving protein powder
1 tablespoon ground flaxseed

Combine all of the ingredients and blend until smooth. Serve right away.

Serves 1 | Per Serving: CALORIES: 413; TOTAL FAT: 13G; SUGAR: 39G; SODIUM: 123MG; CARBOHYDRATES: 63G; FIBER: 8G; PROTEIN: 15G

protein

superfood
star

For a different twist
and richer taste, replace
the frozen banana and
half of the cashews with
½ frozen avocado. You
could also add 1 tablespoon
chocolate chips for
more texture and added
chocolate flavor.

Peppermint Patty

While this smoothie may not taste like a York Peppermint
Patty, it is most certainly better for your health and waistline.
Thanks to the help of the frozen banana and coconut flour,
the consistency of this smoothie is thick and creamy. Cold,
filling, and tasting too sinful to be good, enjoy this superfood
smoothie.

1 cup plain soymilk
¼ cup silken tofu
1 small frozen banana, sliced
1 cup baby spinach
¼ cup cashews, soaked overnight
1 tablespoon coconut flour
1 tablespoon cacao
¼ cup fresh mint leaves
⅛ teaspoon peppermint extract
stevia (optional)
½ to 1 cup ice

Optional Add-Ins:

¼ teaspoon vanilla extract
1 serving protein powder
1 tablespoon coconut sugar
1 tablespoon ground flaxseed

Combine all of the ingredients and blend until smooth.
Serve right away.

Serves 1 | Per Serving: CALORIES: 455; TOTAL FAT: 6G; SUGAR: 21G;
SODIUM: 210MG; CARBOHYDRATES: 52G; FIBER: 11G; PROTEIN: 19G

Blueberry Lavender

When you need an extra dose of calm, try blending up this nutritious deep-purple mix of superfoods. An ingredient in the culinary mix herbes de Provence, dried lavender adds GI health-promoting polyphenols and anxiety-reducing properties to this delicious smoothie.

superfood star

1 cup unsweetened vanilla almond milk
½ cup frozen blueberries
½ frozen banana
2 tablespoons hemp seeds
½ tablespoon dried lavender
½ tablespoon maca powder
1 teaspoon vanilla extract
1 pitted Medjool date
½ to 1 cup ice

Optional Add-Ins:

¼ cup white beans
¼ cup chopped avocado
1 serving protein powder

Combine all of the ingredients and blend until smooth. Serve right away.

You can easily make this into a meal replacement by adding in some oats or quinoa and additional protein such as tofu, beans, Greek yogurt, or powder.

Serves 1 | Per Serving: CALORIES: 326; TOTAL FAT: 10G; SUGAR: 33G; SODIUM: 181MG; CARBOHYDRATES: 52G; FIBER: 8G; PROTEIN: 9G

protein

high
fiber

⬊ Be discerning with
your granola choice and
read the nutrition facts
panel and ingredient list.
Avoid brands that are high
in added sugars and use
partially hydrogenated fats.

Granola Smoothie

Can't decide if you want granola or a smoothie for breakfast?
Why not put them together and enjoy the best of both worlds!
This recipe is highly customizable, so use your favorite protein,
berry, and crunchy cereal. You could also use muesli for a
thicker consistency.

1 cup soy milk
¼ cup low-fat cottage cheese
1 apple, cored and sliced
½ cup frozen cherries
⅓ cup low-fat granola
1 tablespoon chia seeds
½ teaspoon vanilla extract
¼ teaspoon ground cinnamon
1 pitted Medjool date
½ to 1 cup ice

Optional Add-Ins:
1 tablespoon grated coconut
1 tablespoon walnuts
1 tablespoon goji berries
1 tablespoon raisins

Combine all of the ingredients and blend until smooth.
Serve right away.

Serves 1 | Per Serving: CALORIES: 521; TOTAL FAT: 31G; SUGAR: 70G;
SODIUM: 380MG; CARBOHYDRATES: 122G; FIBER: 20G; PROTEIN: 33G

Strawberry Rhubarb Pie

The tart flavor of rhubarb combines with the sweetness of strawberries in this smoothie version of the classic pie. Rhubarb has astounding nutritional value and is packed in fiber, vitamins, minerals, and phytochemicals. The key to this recipe is the fresh and frozen combo, so try to follow as it's written for best results.

1 cup unsweetened vanilla almond milk
½ cup frozen strawberries
½ cup rhubarb slices
½ frozen banana
1 tablespoon ground flaxseed
¼ teaspoon vanilla extract
¼ teaspoon ground cinnamon
stevia (optional)
½ to 1 cup ice

Optional Add-Ins:

1 tablespoon date syrup
½ cup orange juice
½ cup vanilla yogurt

Combine all of the ingredients and blend until smooth. Serve right away.

Serves 1 | Per Serving: CALORIES: 176; TOTAL FAT: 5G; SUGAR: 14G; SODIUM: 183MG; CARBOHYDRATES: 28G; FIBER: 8G; PROTEIN: 3G

low calorie

low sugar

The leaves of rhubarb, cooked or raw, contain toxins that are poisonous, so be certain you discard them. You can buy frozen rhubarb; just choose a brand without added sugar.

protein

high
fiber

For a different
flavor variation, replace
the blackberries with
pineapple, and substitute
pistachios for the almonds.

Blackberry Basil Bliss

With an infusion of the peppery taste of basil, this phytochemical-rich sweet smoothie uses blackberries, avocado, and almonds to create a one-of-a-kind treat. High in bone-building vitamin K, basil is also a potent anti-inflammatory and can help keep cholesterol levels in check.

1 cup soy milk
1 cup frozen blackberries
½ frozen banana
¼ cup chopped avocado
1 cup baby spinach
1 tablespoon almonds
1 teaspoon chia seeds
¼ cup tightly packed basil leaves
½ teaspoon vanilla extract
½ to 1 cup ice

Optional Add-Ins:

¼ cup chopped avocado
1 serving protein powder
1 tablespoon hemp seeds
½ cup frozen mango

Combine all of the ingredients and blend until smooth. Serve right away.

Serves 1 | Per Serving: CALORIES: 380; TOTAL FAT: 16G; SUGAR: 25G; SODIUM: 153MG; CARBOHYDRATES: 50G; FIBER: 15G; PROTEIN: 14G

Key Lime Pie

The official dessert of Key West, Florida, the first key lime pie was created in the 1850s and has been one of America's best-loved regional dishes ever since. This smoothie has the same flavors but is a health-ified remake that you can feel good about enjoying whenever the key lime pie mood strikes.

high protein

1 cup unsweetened almond milk
¾ cup plain Greek yogurt
1 medium frozen banana, sliced
1 tablespoon key lime juice
zest of 1 key lime
½ teaspoon maple syrup
½ to 1 cup ice

For garnish:
1 tablespoon crushed graham crackers
1 tablespoon plain Greek yogurt

Optional Add-Ins:
¼ cup chopped avocado
1 tablespoon ground flaxseed
1 tablespoon hemp seed

Combine all of the ingredients and blend until smooth. Serve right away.

If you can't find key lime juice, you can substitute by making a mixture of ¼ cup fresh lemon juice and ¼ cup fresh lime juice, and then measuring out 1 tablespoon for the recipe.

Serves 1 | Per Serving: CALORIES: 361; TOTAL FAT: 9G; SUGAR: 28G; SODIUM: 286MG; CARBOHYDRATES: 51G; FIBER: 6G; PROTEIN: 15G

protein

superfood
star

This smoothie
is easy to personalize,
depending on how you
like your carrot cake to
taste. Try toasted pecans,
dates, and extra coconut.

Carrot Cake

This smoothie is everything you love about the spicy, fresh-carrot goodness of carrot cake with a bonus: it's good for you! Made with fresh and healthy ingredients, you can feel good about enjoying this dessert-tasting smoothie for breakfast, lunch, snack, or dessert.

⅔ cup almond milk
½ cup Greek yogurt
1 medium frozen banana, sliced
1 cup diced carrots
1 tablespoon shredded coconut
1 tablespoon walnuts
¼ teaspoon ground cinnamon
pinch ground ginger
pinch ground nutmeg
1 teaspoon vanilla extract
2 pitted Medjool dates
½ to 1 cup ice

For Toppings:

extra grated carrots, walnuts, toasted coconut

Optional Add-Ins:

1 tablespoon ground flaxseed
1 tablespoon chia gel
1 teaspoon maple syrup

Combine all of the ingredients and blend until smooth. Serve right away.

Serves 1 | Per Serving: CALORIES: 479; TOTAL FAT: 11G; SUGAR: 61G; SODIUM: 218MG; CARBOHYDRATES: 86G; FIBER: 11G; PROTEIN: 16G

Blueberry Muffin

A fresh and filling breakfast shake reminiscent in flavor of a blueberry muffin, this smoothie is a treat to your taste buds. Soy provides heart-healthy protein while oats and omega-3 fats from chia help you power through a busy morning. So skip the muffin and drink this healthy smoothie instead.

high protein

1 cup soy milk
½ cup frozen blueberries
1 orange, peeled
½ cup rolled oats
2 tablespoons chia seed gel
¼ teaspoon cinnamon
stevia (optional)
½ to 1 cup ice

For more protein and a gluten-free version, replace the rolled oats with ½ cup cooked quinoa, and add ½ cup Greek yogurt, tofu, or a serving of your favorite protein powder.

Optional Add-Ins:

1 teaspoon flax oil
½ cup orange juice
¼ teaspoon lemon zest

Combine all of the ingredients and blend until smooth. Serve right away.

Serves 1 | Per Serving: CALORIES: 432; TOTAL FAT: 8G; SUGAR: 35G; SODIUM: 129MG; CARBOHYDRATES: 77G; FIBER: 13G; PROTEIN: 16G

protein

↘ Adding ¼ to ½ cup
white beans to this
smoothie would boost
the protein, fiber, and B
vitamins while adding a
creamier texture.

Buttermilk Date

Low-fat buttermilk can make a great addition to your smoothie
ingredient repertoire. With a thicker texture than milk, low-fat
buttermilk is low in calories, and high in protein, calcium, and
B vitamins. Sweetened with dates and a touch of honey, this
smoothie makes a quick and nutritious breakfast.

1 cup low-fat buttermilk
1 medium frozen banana, sliced
5 pitted Medjool dates
1 tablespoon chia seed gel
1 tablespoon hemp seed
pinch salt
¼ teaspoon vanilla extract
1 teaspoon honey
½ to 1 cup ice

Optional Add-Ins:

½ cup berries
1 serving protein powder
2 tablespoons almonds

Combine all of the ingredients and blend until smooth.
Serve right away.

Serves 1 | Per Serving: CALORIES: 607; TOTAL FAT: 7G; SUGAR: 112G;
SODIUM: 414MG; CARBOHYDRATES: 136G; FIBER: 12G; PROTEIN: 14G

Blueberry Kale Cacao

With just a hint of cacao, this smoothie is loaded in phytochemicals, vitamins, minerals, fiber, slow-burning carbohydrates, and healthy fats. With protein for added staying power, this smoothie makes a great breakfast or healthy afternoon snack.

1 cup unsweetened protein-fortified vanilla almond milk
½ frozen banana, sliced
½ cup frozen blueberries
2 cups kale
¼ cup rolled oats, soaked
2 tablespoons almonds
1 tablespoon cacao
1 tablespoon chia seeds
1 pitted Medjool date
½ to 1 cup ice

Optional Add-Ins:

1 serving protein powder
¼ cup chopped avocado
½ cup Greek yogurt

Combine all of the ingredients and blend until smooth. Serve right away.

Serves 1 | Per Serving: CALORIES: 453; TOTAL FAT: 14G; SUGAR: 32G; SODIUM: 241MG; CARBOHYDRATES: 80G; FIBER: 16G; PROTEIN: 14G

high
protein

superfood
star

high
fiber

 Try soaking your oats, almonds, and chia together in the almond milk overnight for a thicker, creamier shake. You could also substitute the oats with quinoa for added protein.

You can replace
the pumpkin and
sunflower seeds with
equal amounts of walnuts
and/or almonds, which
are also good sources of
magnesium.

Slumber with Seeds and Cherries

Too little sleep can increase your levels of cortisol and promote harmful belly fat, which has been linked to chronic disease, but the good news is there are many sleep-promoting foods. Cherries contain melatonin, seeds contain muscle-relaxing magnesium, cottage cheese and bananas contain tryptophan, and complex carbs increase serotonin levels. Here's to a good night's sleep.

½ cup unsweetened vanilla almond milk
½ cup cottage cheese
1 frozen banana, sliced
½ cup frozen cherries
¼ cup rolled oats, soaked
1 tablespoon pumpkin seeds
1 tablespoon sunflower seeds
1 tablespoon chamomile flowers
1 teaspoon vanilla extract
stevia (optional)
½ to 1 cup ice

Optional Add-Ins:

½ cup 100% tart cherry juice
1 tablespoon ground flaxseed
¼ cup canned pumpkin

Combine all of the ingredients and blend until smooth. Serve right away.

Serves 1 | Per Serving: CALORIES: 415; TOTAL FAT: 11G; SUGAR: 23G; SODIUM: 554MG; CARBOHYDRATES: 57G; FIBER: 8G; PROTEIN: 23G

Raspberry Mint

Simple, sweet, and nutritious, this probiotic-rich smoothie uses phytochemical-rich raspberries with just a touch of mint to create a digestion-promoting drink. Raspberries have one of the most diverse sets of antioxidant and anti-inflammatory phytonutrients among fruits. This smoothie is a refreshing snack that combats obesity and helps lower blood sugar.

½ cup unsweetened vanilla almond milk
½ cup Greek yogurt
1 cup frozen raspberries
½ frozen banana
1 tablespoon chia seeds
1 tablespoon fresh mint
stevia (optional)
½ to 1 cup ice

Optional Add-Ins:

¼ cup chopped avocado
1 pitted Medjool date
2 tablespoons almonds

Combine all of the ingredients and blend until smooth. Serve right away.

Serves 1 | Per Serving: CALORIES: 512; TOTAL FAT: 9G; SUGAR: 70G; SODIUM: 160MG; CARBOHYDRATES: 91G; FIBER: 16G; PROTEIN: 25G

high
protein

high
fiber

Buy raspberries when they are in season and freeze them for future use. Wash them gently and pat with a paper towel, arrange on a flat pan and freeze, and once frozen, transfer to a plastic freezer bag.

The Dirty Dozen and the Clean Fifteen

2015	
DIRTY DOZEN	**CLEAN FIFTEEN**
Apples	Asparagus
Celery	Avocados
Cherry tomatoes	Cabbage
Cucumbers	Cantaloupe
Grapes	Cauliflower
Nectarines	Eggplant
Peaches	Grapefruit
Potatoes	Kiwis
Snap peas	Mangos
Spinach	Onions
Strawberries	Papayas
Sweet bell peppers	Pineapples
In addition to the Dirty Dozen, the EWG added two foods contaminated with highly toxic organo-phosphate insecticides:	Sweet corn
	Sweet peas (frozen)
	Sweet potatoes
Hot peppers	
Kale/Collard greens	

A nonprofit and environmental watchdog organization called Environmental Working Group (EWG) looks at data supplied by the US Department of Agriculture (USDA) and the Food and Drug Administration (FDA) about pesticide residues and compiles a list each year of the best and worst pesticide loads found in commercial crops. You can refer to the Dirty Dozen list to know which fruits and vegetables you should always buy organic. The Clean Fifteen list lets you know which produce is considered safe enough when grown conventionally to allow you to skip the organics. This does not mean that the Clean Fifteen produce is pesticide-free, though, so wash these fruits and vegetables thoroughly. These lists change every year, so make sure you look up the most recent before you fill your shopping cart. You'll find the most recent lists as well as a guide to pesticides in produce at www.EWG.org/FoodNews.

Glossary

alkalinity: A pH measures how acid or alkaline something is. A pH of 0 is totally acidic, while a pH of 14 is completely alkaline, and a pH of 7.0 is neutral. Your blood is slightly alkaline and your stomach very acidic. Most fruits and vegetables, soybeans, tofu, and some nuts and seeds are alkaline promoting, which is supposed to decrease risk for disease. Processed foods and meats are said to be acid-forming and increase risk.

amino acid: The 20 building blocks of proteins.

antioxidant: A substance that reduces damage due to oxygen, such as that caused by free radicals.

beta-carotene: A vitamin that acts as an antioxidant; found in dark green, yellow, and orange fruits and vegetables and converted to vitamin A in the body.

carotenoid: Yellow, orange, or red fat-soluble pigments that give color to fruit and vegetables, and are converted to vitamin A in the body.

catechin: A powerful anti-inflammatory phytochemical.

choline: A B vitamin important for neurotransmitter function, particularly its role in memory and learning.

CoQ_{10}: A nutrient that is an antioxidant made by the body that helps produce energy, neutralize free radicals, and may even improve athletic performance.

demulcent: A food that coats and soothes the stomach.

EGCG (epigallocatechin gallate): The main antioxidant in green tea.

electrolyte: A substance such as sodium or calcium that regulates the flow of nutrients into, and wastes out of, cells.

enzyme: A protein that acts as a catalyst and speeds up reactions in the body without getting changed in the process. Specific enzymes help digest proteins, fats, and carbohydrates.

fiber: The parts of fruits and vegetables that cannot be digested.

flavonoids: A large class of water-soluble pigments found in foods that act as antioxidants.

free radical: An atom or group of atoms with an unpaired electron that can damage cells.

gums: Polysaccharides produced by the fermentation of carbohydrates that act as thickening agents.

lauric acid: An antiviral compound.

lycopene: An antioxidant that can protect DNA from damage.

maca: A superfood noted for its ability to increase stamina and boost energy.

monounsaturated fat content: A type of fat that can keep brain cell membranes flexible.

omega-3 fat: A type of polyunsaturated fat that is considered to be essential and must be obtained through the diet.

phytochemicals: Also called phytonutrient, they are naturally occurring compounds in plants (*phyto* means plant in Greek). Some are responsible for the colors of our fruits and vegetables but they all have health-promoting properties, such as lycopene in tomatoes, which decreases the risk of prostate cancer.

polyphenol: An antioxidant phytochemical that tends to prevent or neutralize the damaging effects of free radicals.

prebiotic: A nondigestible food ingredient that promotes the growth of beneficial microorganisms in the intestines.

precursor: An inactive substance that converts to an active one, such as a vitamin.

probiotic: Live bacteria in yogurt and other cultured foods that promote the growth of beneficial bacteria in the intestines.

purine: One of two classes of DNA and RNA found in all of the body's cells and virtually all foods.

resveratrol: A class of polyphenols found in certain plants that has antioxidant properties.

serotonin: A neurotransmitter involved in the control of pain perception, the sleep-wake cycle, and mood.

tryptophan: An essential amino acid and component of proteins; necessary for growth.

uric acid: A byproduct of the breakdown of purines in foods.

whole foods: Unprocessed foods such as fresh fruits and vegetables, lean meats, minimally processed soy, and dairy products.

References

American Heart Association. "About Sodium (Salt)." Last modified November 11, 2014. www.heart.org/HEARTORG/GettingHealthy/NutritionCenter/HealthyEating/About-Sodium-Salt_UCM_463416_Article.jsp.

Calbom, Cherie. *The Ultimate Smoothie Book: 130 Delicious Recipes for Blender Drinks, Frozen Desserts, Shakes and More.* New York: Grand Central Life & Style, 2006.

Castle, Kirk. *100 Healthy Smoothie Recipes.* Amazon: CreateSpace, 2013.

Chace, Danielle. *More Smoothies for Life: Satisfy, Energize, and Heal Your Body.* New York: Clarkson Potter, 2007.

Daniels, Emma. *Vegan Smoothie Recipes: The Delicious, Weight Loss & Healthy Living Vegan Smoothie Recipe Book.* Amazon: CreateSpace, 2014.

Dobbins, Lee Anne. *Healthy Smoothie Recipes: Healthy Herbal Smoothies that are Nutritious, Delicious and Easy to Make.* Amazon: CreateSpace, 2012.

Garden-Robinson, Julie. "What Color Is Your Food?" North Dakota State University. Last modified May 2011. www.ag.ndsu.edu/pubs/yf/foods/fn595.pdf.

Hajhashemi, V., G. Vaseghi, M. Pourfarzam, and A. Abdollahi. "Are Antioxidants Helpful for Disease Prevention?" *Research in Pharmaceutical Sciences* 5, no. 1 (2010 Jan-Jun): 1–8. www.ncbi.nlm.nih.gov/pmc/articles/PMC3093095/.

Joyner, Nadia. *Green Smoothies. 50+ Recipes for Nutrition, Life and Health.* Amazon: CreateSpace, 2013.

King D. E., A. G. Mainous 3rd, C. A. Lambourne. "Trends in Dietary Fiber Intake in the United States, 1999–2008." *Journal of the Academy of Nutrition and Dietetics* 112, no. 9 (May 2012): 642-8. doi:10.1016/j.jand.2012.01.019.

Mayo Clinic. "Dietary Fiber: Essential for a Healthy Diet." Accessed on August 3, 2015. www.mayoclinic.org/healthy-lifestyle/nutrition-and-healthy-eating/in-depth/fiber/art-20043983.

MedLine Plus. "Antioxidants." Last modified July 31, 2015. www.nlm.nih.gov/medlineplus/antioxidants.html.

Mendocino Press. *The Smoothie Recipe Book for Beginners: Essential Smoothies to Get Healthy, Lose Weight, Feel Great.* Berkeley. CA: Mendocino Press, 2014.

Morris, Julie. *Superfood Smoothies: 100 Delicious, Energizing & Nutrient Dense Recipes.* New York: Sterling Publishing, 2013.

Nicklas, Theresa A., Lisa Jahns, Margaret L. Bogle, and Deirdra N. Chester, et al. "Barriers and Facilitators for Consumer Adherence to the Dietary Guidelines for Americans: The HEALTH Study." *Journal of the Academy of Nutrition and Dietetics* 113 (October 2013): 1317-31. doi:http://dx.doi.org/10.1016/j.jand.2013.05/004.

Paul, Tamara. *Gluten-Free Smoothie Recipes.* Amazon: CreateSpace, 2014.

Roberts, Kasia. *The Superfood Smoothie Recipe Book: Super-Nutritious, High-Protein Smoothies to Lose Weight, Boost Metabolism and Increase Energy.* Amazon: CreateSpace, 2014.

Rockridge Press. *Green Smoothies for Beginners: Essentials to Get Started.* Berkeley, CA: Callisto Media, 2013.

Rockridge Press. *The Smoothie Recipe Book: 150 Recipes Including Recipes for Weight Loss and Smoothies for Optimum Health.* Berkeley, CA: Callisto Media, 2013.

Sharpe, Diane. *The Fat Burner Smoothies: The Recipe Book of Fat Burning Superfood Smoothies for Weight Loss and Smoothies for Good Health.* Amazon: CreateSpace, 2014.

Sparks, Ariel. *Sugar-Free Green Smoothie Recipes.* Amazon: CreateSpace, 2014.

Swann-Miller, Liz. *The New Green Smoothie Diet Solution: Nature's Fast Lane to Peak Health.* Amazon: CreateSpace, 2012.

"Vitamin & Supplements Center: Search for a Vitamin or Supplement." WebMD. Accessed August 4, 2015. www.webmd.com/vitamins-supplements/default.aspx.

"What Are the Benefits of Cayenne?" MNT (Medical News Today). Last modified September 8, 2014. www.medicalnewstoday.com/articles/267248.php.

Recipe Index

Recipe Label Index

green smoothie

Beet Cherry Detox, 38
Blueberry Kombucha, 115
Carrot Kale Detox, 41
Cilantro Mango Smoothie, 33
Ginger Watermelon Detox, 34
Gorgeous Green Grape, 125
Immune Supporting Mango Ginger, 109
Kiwi Cleanser, 39
Lean, Mean, and Dandelion Green, 121
Lemon-Lime Spinach Cleanser, 31
Minty Apple Fennel, 35
Nectarine Naturally Glowing, 129
Parsley Power, 145
Pear Ginger Digestion Booster, 81
Pineapple Watercress Green Tea, 37
Slimming Greens and Herbs, 71
Timeless Tea Toner, 128

high fiber

Açai Apple Avocado, 162
Almond Joint Joy, 142
Apple Cherry Pumpkin Tea, 133
Berry Metabolism Booster, 64
Blackberry Basil Bliss, 174
Blackberry Stomach Support, 84
Blueberry Banana Cocoa Bean, 161
Blueberry Kale Cacao, 179
Blueberry Kombucha, 115
Cashew Cream, 149
Chipper Cherry Ginger, 117
Chocolate Cocoa Pinto Bean, 104
Clementine Cholesterol Crusher, 155
Crunchy Nutty Goji Berry, 151
Feel Good Flax and Fiber, 160
Gorgeous Green Grape, 125
Granola Smoothie, 172
Green Tea and Vegetable Smoothie, 73
Java Delight, 102
Jicama Hemp Immune Support, 120
Kiwi Cleanser, 39
Kiwi Spinach Chia, 57
Mango White Bean, 65
Minty Apple Fennel, 35
Orange Broccoli Bone Builder, 147
Orange Omegas, 163
Peanut Butter Immune Builder, 112
Peanut Butter Raspberry, 66
Raspberry Mint, 181

Raspberry Zinc Zinger, 114
Rejuvenating Orange Strawberry, 40
Restorative Raspberry, 47
Strawberry Kefir Stomach Soother, 85
Tropical Kiwi Pineapple Protein, 72

high protein

Açai Apple Avocado, 162
Ageless Avocado, 126
Almond Joint Joy, 142
Apple Cashew, 63
Apple Cherry Pumpkin Tea, 133
Apricot Avenger, 141
Apricot Cottage Cheese, 67
Avocado Banana Soothing Smoothie, 80
Balancing Blueberry, 48
Beauty with Berries and Beets, 132
Beet Cranberry Crusher, 146
Beet Raspberry Kale, 94
Berry Brain Booster, 95
Berry Heart Healthy, 156
Berry Metabolism Booster, 64
Blackberry Basil Bliss, 174
Blackberry Stomach Support, 84
Blueberry Banana Cocoa Bean, 161
Blueberry Basil Anti-Inflammatory, 51
Blueberry Ginger Joint Ease, 150
Blueberry Kale Cacao, 179
Blueberry Mango Bean, 134
Blueberry Muffin, 177

low calorie

Index

CPSIA information can be obtained
at www.ICGtesting.com
Printed in the USA
BVHW02s0751220318
511186BV00011B/273/P